LONG TERM OUTLOOK FOR THE WORLD AUTOMOBILE INDUSTRY

ORGANISATION FOR ECONOMIC CO-OPERATION AND DEVELOPMENT

Pursuant to article 1 of the Convention signed in Paris on 14th December, 1960, and which came into force on 30th September, 1961, the Organisation for Economic Co-operation and Development (OECD) shall promote policies designed:

- to achieve the highest sustainable economic growth and employment and a rising standard of living in Member countries, while maintaining financial stability, and thus to contribute to the development of the world economy;
- to contribute to sound economic expansion in Member as well as non-member countries in the process of economic development; and
- to contribute to the expansion of world trade on a multilateral, non-discriminatory basis in accordance with international obligations.

The Signatories of the Convention on the OECD are Austria, Belgium, Canada, Denmark, France, the Federal Republic of Germany, Greece, Iceland, Ireland, Italy, Luxembourg, the Netherlands, Norway, Portugal, Spain, Sweden, Switzerland, Turkey, the United Kingdom and the United States. The following countries acceded subsequently to this Convention (the dates are those on which the instruments of accession were deposited): Japan (28th April, 1964), Finland (28th January, 1969), Australia (7th June, 1971) and New Zealand (29th May, 1973).

The Socialist Federal Republic of Yugoslavia takes part in certain work of the OECD (agreement of 28th October, 1961).

Publié en français sous le titre:

PERSPECTIVES A LONG TERME
DE L'INDUSTRIE AUTOMOBILE
MONDIALE

As the Industry Committee recommended when deciding to implement this work, the study deals with the long-term perspectives of the automobile industry (1990-2000). It is however obvious that, even in such a framework, current problems cannot be overlooked; they have thus been placed in a global long-term context. The objective throughout the study has been to indicate possible trends and to analyse some factors which form their basis. It aims to indicate areas where problems could arise and on which governments should reflect together.

Also available

INDUSTRIAL ROBOTS: their Impact and Diffusion in Manufacturing Industry (forthcoming)
(70 83 02 1) ISBN 92-64-12486-1 £4.90 US$9.75 F49.00

INDUSTRY IN TRANSITION: Experience of the 70s and Prospects for the 80s. "Document" Series (July 1983)
(70 83 01 1) ISBN 92-64-12469-1 236 pages £8.50 US$17.00 F85.00

TEXTILE AND CLOTHING INDUSTRIES: Structural Problems and Policies in OECD Countries (May 1983)
(71 83 70 1) ISBN 92-64-12432-2 176 pages £7.00 US$14.00 F70.00

TELECOMMUNICATIONS: Pressures and Policies for Change (april 1983)
(93 83 02 1) ISBN 92-64-12428-4 142 pages £6.90 US$14.00 F69.00

Prices charged at the OECD Publications Office.

THE OECD CATALOGUE OF PUBLICATIONS and supplements will be sent free of charge on request addressed either to OECD Publications Office,
2, rue André-Pascal, 75775 PARIS CEDEX 16, or to the OECD Sales Agent in your country.

TABLE OF CONTENTS

Chapter I

INTRODUCTION

This study has two basic objectives: to consider the probable long-term outlook for the world automobile industry and to assess its implications for policy.

Following an Introduction outlining the recent situation, Chapters II and III concentrate on the main factors likely to affect demand and supply in the world motor industry over the next two decades. A final chapter draws some conclusions concerning the policies which might be suitable.

Economic importance of the industry

A brief description is given below of the key role of the automobile industry, mainly in the economies of the OECD countries.

Sales

World sales of cars, which had reached some 28 million units in 1980 (3 million more than in 1979) were widely disappointing in 1981 and 1982. OECD countries account for approximately 80 per cent of total world sales. The world car market has been estimated at approximately US$250 billion (based on an average price of US$9,000 per car); this is equivalent to the GDP of a country such as Canada. Adding on sales of parts and second-hand vehicles and turnover on repair work could well increase total sales generated by the car industry by 100 to 150 per cent.

In 1981 and 1982, sales of new vehicles declined in most markets, and there are very few countries where the motor industry has been able to achieve its production, profit or employment targets. Very often this has meant reductions in working hours, lay-offs and even factory closures, as in the case of British Leyland, GM and Ford. The decline in sales is not confined to North America or Europe: even in countries previously considered to be growth markets, such as Mexico and Brazil, sales have gone down significantly.

Whilst there is no way of classifying them by order of importance, the factors which have particularly affected the market in the majority of countries in recent years include the broad decline in incomes as a result of the widespread economic recession, erosion of consumers' confidence, changes in government economic policies, higher motor fuel prices, high interest rates, the higher cost of buying and running a vehicle, etc. Chapter II forecasts growth in vehicle demand to 1990-2000, and lists the main factors influencing present and future demand.

Production

Some 28 million vehicles were produced in 1981. This was 4 per cent lower than in 1980 and 12 per cent lower than in 1978, a record world production year. Table 1 below shows trends in world production since 1960. In 1981, the leading producer countries

Table 1. Production by country of passenger vehicles

Unit '000s

	1960	1965	1975	1976	1977	1978	1979	1980	1981	1982
F.R. Germany	1 817	2 734	2 908	3 547	3 790	3 890	3 932	3 521	3 578	3 761
Belgium	194	(200)	793	1 040	1 054	1 053	1 029	882	852	950
France	1 175	1 341	2 546	2 979	3 092	3 111	3 220	2 939	2 612	2 777
Italy	596	1 104	1 348	1 471	1 440	1 509	1 481	1 445	1 257	1 297
Netherlands	(20)	60	71	86	68	69	90	81	78	86
United Kingdom	1 353	1 722	1 268	1 333	1 328	1 223	1 070	924	955	888
EEC	5 155	7 161	8 934	10 456	10 772	10 855	10 822	9 792	9 332	9 759
Spain	43	180	696	753	989	986	966	1 029	855	928
Sweden	108	182	316	317	235	254	297	235	258	295
Others	8	32	62	136	131	95	27	(30)	(40)	(50)
Europe OECD	5 314	7 555	10 008	11 662	12 127	12 190	12 112	11 086	10 485	11 032
Japan	165	696	4 568	5 028	5 431	5 976	6 176	7 038	6 974	6 887
United-States	6 675	9 335	6 717	8 498	9 214	9 176	8 434	6 377	6 280	4 974
Canada	323	709	1 058	1 150	1 166	1 162	989	847	744	807
Australia	125	304	283	292	253	289	405	317	352	371
Total OECD	12 602	18 599	22 634	26 630	28 191	28 793	28 116	25 665	24 853	24 071
Comecon	264	299	1 540	1 608	1 739	1 812	1 846	1 865	2 247	(2 189)
of which :										
URSS	..	196	1 201	1 200	1 280	1 312	1 314	1 330	1 324	1 325
Czechoslovakia	..	78	175	179	159	175	182	184	171	182
Poland	..	25	164	229	300	325	350	351	248	208
Latin America	133	205	1 323	1 357	1 290	(1 044)	(1 373)	(1 417)	901	(1 126)
Others	..	..	359	443	314	(115)	(190)	(244)	111	137
World	12 999	19 103	25 856	29 152	30 906	31 764	31 525	29 191	(28 094)	(27 500)

8

were Japan and the United States, each of which accounted for approximately 23 per cent of world production; and the six main producing countries of the European Communities (which jointly turned out 33 per cent of world production).

Production has long been in the hands of a relatively restricted number of manufacturers, particularly in the United States and Japan. In each of these countries, the two largest firms respectively control 84 per cent (GM and Ford US) and 59 per cent (Toyota and Nissan) of the domestic market. In Europe a similar position is shared by five firms. Table 2 lists the main world car manufacturers producing over 500 000 units in 1980 and 1981.

Table 2. **Leading world manufacturers of passenger vehicles[1]**

	Production 1980	Production 1981
General Motors[2]	5 713 343	5 499 330
Ford	3 066 278	3 097 249
Toyota[3]	2 458 888	2 395 390
Nissan[4]	2 193 653	2 105 702
Volkswagen Audi	2 280 093	2 023 614
Renault	1 874 008	1 607 818
Peugeot-Citroën-Talbot	1 748 763	1 579 193
Fiat[5]	1 379 242	1 171 544
Chrysler	766 504	869 797
Honda	845 515	852 177
Toyo Kogyo (Mazda)	736 544	840 630

1. More than 500 000 passenger vehicles produced - COMECON excluded.
2. Includes Opel and Vauxhall.
3. Includes Daihatsu.
4. Includes Fuji (Subaru).
5. Includes Autobianchi, Lancia and Ferrari.

International trade

Table 3 shows, in matrix form, world trade in 1981 for finished cars. There are no data on trade between non-OECD countries (mainly Member countries of the CMEA). The world figure, however, may be put at something like US$60 billion.

The leading exporters of finished vehicles in 1981 were Japan (with 30.7 per cent of the world total), FR Germany (22.8 per cent), France (9.2 per cent), Belgium (7.0 per cent) and the United States and Canada (6.7 per cent and 7.6 per cent respectively). The United States is a major importer taking over 30 per cent of total world imports. A major importing region was the EEC, nearly 30 per cent of the world total (and about half of this total being intra-EEC trade). The situation in 1981, as in previous years, may be summed up as follows: the United States was a net importer, Europe and Japan were net exporters. In Japan, the share of production exported was particularly high, being some 50 per cent or more.

International trade in parts is also very considerable. World exports in 1980 are estimated at approximately US$31.6 billion. The leading exporters of parts are the EEC (US$17.2 billion, i.e. around 54 per cent of the world total), the United States (US$8.7 billion, around 25 per cent), Canada (US$2.7 billion, around 9 per cent) and Japan (US$2.2 billion, around 7 per cent).

The importance of the motor industry in international world trade is clear. In 1980, international trade in road vehicles represented 15.5 per cent of world trade in the manufacturing industry – and this figure does not include trade in parts, engines and tyres. The industry is a major factor in the balance of payments of the main producing countries. In 1980, United States automobile exports accounted for some 12 per cent of

9

Table 3. **World trade in cars 1981**

Millions US$

Exports from / to	United States	EEC	Total OECD	Non-OECD	World
Canada	4 211	8	4 224	327	4 551
United States	–	93	3 353	673	4 026
FR Germany	2 665	7 402	12 631	1 066	13 697
France	314	3 141	4 024	1 498	5 523
Italy	139	900	1 306	312	1 619
United Kingdom	299	553	1 006	769	1 774
BLEU	3	3 726	4 104	78	4 182
Other EEC	1	388	470	29	499
Total EEC	3 421	16 110	23 541	9 752	27 294
Japan	9 542	2 475	14 508	3 938	18 445
Sweden	584	127	1 166	96	1 262
Total OECD	17 760	20 237	48 169	8 959	57 128

Notes :
  i) The totals may not tally exactly because of the rounded figures.
  ii) Data based on fob export values for finished cars.
Source : OECD, Statistics of Foreign Trade 1981, item SITC, Rev. 2, No. 781.0.

that country's exports of manufactured products; percentages for Japan, France and FR Germany are approximately 25, 18 and 19 per cent respectively. Similarly, motor vehicle imports represent a significant proportion of manufactured (and total) imports for some countries. For example, they represent about 20 per cent of the US's manufactured imports and over 10 per cent of the UK's.

Trade relations in recent years in the motor vehicle sector have greatly deteriorated, mainly because of the weakening demand in the United States and Europe and the changing attitude of consumers. These factors will be examined in subsequent chapters. The United States and Canada have experienced mounting imports of small cars with better fuel consumption performance. ThUs it was considered that Japanese producers, the main exporters, ought voluntarily to limit exports to these markets so that the US and Canadian industries could restructure in sound conditions and as rapidly as possible. In several European countries (including the United Kingdom, France, Italy and Belgium), too, imports of Japanese cars have been limited, sometimes on a voluntary basis.

Employment

The motor industry's share of total manufacturing industry employment[1] in 1980 was approximately 10.4 per cent in FR Germany, 9.6 per cent in France, 7.9 per cent in Sweden, 5.8 per cent in the United Kingdom, 4.3 per cent in the United States and 8.9 per cent in Japan. In general, these percentages are a few points below the corresponding value-added figures, which would suggest productivity and/or capital intensiveness are slightly higher than in manufacturing industry as a whole. Since 1980, the employment situation has deteriorated significantly in most motor manufacturing countries. This trend raises the question of whether the recent lay-offs are structural or cyclical in nature.

Table 4 below shows the employment situation in since 1978 in some of the main world's biggest motor manufacturers.

1 Item 3843 ISIC "Motor Vehicles"
Source: OECD, Indicators of Industrial Activity; 1981.

10

Table 4. **Employment trends in some of the world's biggest motor manufacturers**

	1978	1979	1980	1981
General Motors	839 000	853 000	746 000	741 000
Toyota	45 200	45 230	47 060	56 000
Nissan	55 750	56 700	56 284[2]	
Volkswagen Audi	207 000	240 000	257 930	247 000
Ford	506 500	494 600	426 740	404 790
PSA Peugeot-Citroën-Talbot	160 110	264 730[1]	245 000	218 000
Renault RVI	143 030	141 450	134 790	131 780
Fiat (automobiles)	133 514	139 000	134 000	123 607
Toyo Kogyo (Mazda)	27 827	26 809	27 474	27 500

1. New structure from 1979.
2. June 1981.
Note : These figures only intend to show trends within individual companies. Given the wide differences in the structures of the companies and the definitions used, no comparisons should be made between companies or countries, and no conclusion should thus be drawn from any comparison.
Source : Companies' reports.

Structure

In the early years of this century, the motor manufacturing industry at world level was highly concentrated. During the years of expansion in the 1920s and 1930s, the number of producers increased steeply. Thereafter, and up to the 1970s, the return to industrial concentration was mainly the result of competitive pressures at domestic level.

In more recent years, international pressure has been the main determinant of structural change. The increase in concentration and co-operation, and hence in the accompanying structuring and rationalisation measures, has followed different paths in the main world producing centres.

In Western Europe, concentration was a response first to competition from other European producers (including Ford, General Motors and Chrysler subsidiaries) and, more recently, to Japanese imports. The concentration generally took place within the various producer countries. In the United Kingdom, the main non-American firms joined forces in British Leyland. Other examples are the Volkswagen-Audi, Peugeot-Citroën-Talbot, and Fiat groups. Plant specialisation has increased, so as to gain further economies of scale.

In 1920, there were some 80 automobile producers in the United States. The degree of concentration subsequently increased steeply (30 producers in 1930 and approximately 9 in 1950); today, the three largest producers are responsible for almost 95 per cent of the country's car production. Obviously, the main reason for this trend has been the search for economies of scale – at the cost, perhaps, of some of the industry's flexibility. While in recent years there has been no significant change with regard to concentration, major adjustments have been made in overseas operations particularly in Europe and in the Pacific region.

Concentration has also grown in Japan. In that country, many small producers have established links with the two major producers, Toyota and Nissan.

This trend towards concentration has been accompanied by growth in co-operation between manufacturers through the establishment of joint technical, marketing and production set-ups. Examples are the links between General Motors and Isuzu, Chrysler and Mitsubishi, Ford and Toyo-Kogyo, Renault and American Motors.

A third, similar, development which has become particularly important recently is cost-sharing in research and development. Peugeot, Renault and Volvo, for example, are co-operating in engine design and production in a jointly-owned factory in France; and Fiat and Peugeot are collaborating on the production of a small engine. (Producers in OECD countries and producers in East European countries have also made a number of agreements recently.)

There are three reasons for the increasing internationalisation of the industry: the founding of the European Economic Community; the growth of motor exports from Japan; and the considerable possibilities opened up by the industrial development and advantageous production costs of the newly-industrialising countries. There is no doubt that these factors have greatly altered the nature of motor manufacturing and rendered analysis of future trends more complex. Chapters III and IV look at selected supply aspects in more detail.

There are also considerable differences between the United States, Japan and Europe with regard to the structure of the motor parts industry. A 1980 study by the Commission of the European Communities finds that the Japanese motor parts industry is much more concentrated than the EEC's: there are some 350 parts manufacturers in Japan, compared to 1,750 in Europe. The size of parts firms is distinctly larger in the United States and Japan than in Europe, and their financial and industrial ties at the domestic level are also much closer.

Until recently, the financial situation of most of the world's motor firms was fundamentally sound: self-financing was the main, and sometimes only, source of investment for most motor manufacturers. However, in the years from 1980 through 1982, as demand fell and international competition increased on all markets, many companies' financial positions deteriorated badly. In some countries, governments had to intervene to prevent some firms from going bankrupt (e.g. Chrysler and British Leyland). The decline in demand occurred at a time when manufacturers were launching ambitious programmes of investment and renovation to meet the new challenges arising from the energy crisis and the increased internationalisation of competition. Between 1978 and 1985, American manufacturers intend to invest some $80 billion in re-equipping their factories. In Europe, the cost of manufacturers' projects over this same period are estimated at $35 billion; and in Japan, between 1980 and 1983, they are expected to be of the order of $12 billion. Some of these programmes recently have been scaled down, e.g. those of General Motors and Ford in the United States and of Peugeot in France. This retrenching raises a problem for governments and state financing agencies, which have to consider their policy orientations in relation to the financing of this crucial investment.

This brief introduction has underlined some main features of recent trends in the motor industry at world level and in the main OECD producer countries. Other important developments such as government intervention, trade restrictions, and localisation will be discussed later in the report. The study will also attempt to sketch possible future trends in the world industry beginning in Chapter II with an assessment of the long-term outlook for demand.

Chapter II

FUTURE TRENDS IN DEMAND

Important Note

The conclusions of Chapter II on the possible demand for cars in the 1980s and 1990s should only be considered as broad indications calculated by the Secretariat. They do not necessarily represent the agreed views of individual countries. Generally speaking, however, the Secretariat's projections appear to indicate a reasonable order of magnitude for most countries, although they may be seen as somewhat conservative for some countries. Furthermore, in many projections of the automobile market, the calculated growth potential is underestimated for countries which are highly motorised, and often overestimated in countries with a low degree of motorisation.

Introduction

In 1980, the world passenger automobile market, as measured by new registrations, totalled approximately 28 million units. The OECD area accounted for around 23 million units or about 82 per cent of this total market.

New registrations in the OECD area in 1980 were down by about 8 per cent compared to 1979 because of a drop in demand in all major OECD markets except Italy (see Table 5). Moreover, preliminary data for 1981 indicate a further weakening in automobile demand in the OECD area.

Many of the current difficulties can be ascribed to cyclical factors, but there are structural factors at work too. One such element is a general loss of market dynamism as OECD markets approach saturation levels; demand growth is thus increasingly

Table 5. **New registrations of passenger cars, OECD area[1], 1960-1980**

Million units

	1960	1965	1970	1975	1979	1980	1981
Germany	0.97	1.52	2.11	2.11	2.62	2.43	2.33
France	0.64	1.06	1.30	1.48	1.98	1.87	1.84
U.K.	0.81	1.15	1.08	1.20	1.72	1.51	1.49
Italy	0.38	0.89	1.36	1.06	1.43	1.72	1.74
USA	6.58	9.31	8.39	8.26	10.33	8.76	6.25
Canada	0.50[2]	0.71	0.93	1.06	1.00	0.93	(0.94)
Japan	0.12	0.51	2.38	2.74	3.04	2.85	2.87
Other OECD	0.90[2]	1.65[1]	2.18	2.76	2.91	3.08	2.84
Total OECD	10.90[2]	16.80[2]	19.33	20.67	25.03	25.15	(20.30)

1. Excludes Greece, Ireland, Turkey and New Zealand.
2. Estimate.
Source : l'*Argus*, Chambre Syndicale des Constructeurs d'automobiles.

becoming a function of replacement rather than new (first-time) demand. This trend, which became apparent during the early 1970s in the more developed OECD automobile markets has picked up momentum and spread to other markets in the OECD area. Chiefly as a result of this influence, automobile demand growth in the OECD area fell from an annual rate of 6.1 per cent in the 1960s to around 1.6 per cent in the 1970s.

A return in the next two decades to 1960s-type demand growth is unlikely, since it would require either a marked speeding-up along the approach path to theoretical saturation levels, or an upward shift in the saturation levels themselves. This, in turn, would require substantial increases in real income relative to motoring costs, or fundamental changes in the concept of the automobile. Such possibilities do not seem likely within the period under review. The only other possibility for sizeable demand growth in the OECD area (say of 4-5 per cent per annum over the long-term) would be a decrease in vehicle lifetimes, leading to higher scrapping rates of the vehicle stock. This is also unlikely; on present evidence the reverse could possibly occur.

On the other hand, considerable potential exists for market expansion outside the OECD area. Automobile markets in a number of the developing countries are now reaching the growth or "diffusion" stage, and will thus account for an increasing share of the world market over the medium to long term. However, since the developing country markets will be growing from a low base, their share of the world automobile market will continue, at least in medium term, to be significantly less than that occupied by OECD markets.

This Chapter is in two parts. Part 1 contains a general discussion of the main determinants of automobile demand in a long-term context. The difficulties of measuring the effect of many of these influences are considerable; hence the Secretariat has adopted a relatively simple forecasting method in order to sketch a scenario of world automobile demand by 1990 and the year 2000. Part 2 outlines the main features of this scenario, and discusses some conclusions and policy implications arising from the projected demand developments.

1. DETERMINANTS OF AUTOMOBILE DEMAND

The factors which influence automobile demand are many and complex. Their significance can vary widely between vehicle classes, socio-economic groups and countries. Some determinants also have a distinctly short-term effect (e.g. cost of credit) whereas others are more discernible over the long term (e.g. land-use patterns, traffic congestion, general attitudes to car ownership). The more important variables are briefly discussed below.

A. Demographic factors

Population growth obviously underpins growth in automobile demand over the long term. Since the aggregate population of the OECD area is forecast[1] to increase by 12 per cent in absolute terms over the 1980-2000 period, automobile demand should be at least this much higher, irrespective of the anticipated growth in the number of vehicles per head of population[2].

---

1. *"World Population Trends and Prospects by Country"*, 1950-2000, United Nations, 1979. For a few countries, the UN forecasts for population growth could have been overestimated.
2. And assuming that the "car-driving" population increases by the same proportion as the total population.

Outside the OECD area, the absolute population increase between 1980-2000 is forecast by the United Nations at around 46 per cent. The main growth areas should be Africa (77 per cent), Latin America (65 per cent) and Asia (43 per cent). Assuming that it does not create an economic drag on the countries involved, population growth of this magnitude will contribute substantially to growth of demand for automobiles.

Household characteristics will also influence both aggregate demand and the pattern of demand for automobiles. It is not proposed to examine here the likely effects of various factors under this heading. Nevertheless, it is instructive to note the main elements as seen by Bates and Roberts[3] in a cross-sectional context:

- economies of scale resulting from shared travel;
- the role of the automobile in assisting the journey to work;
- factors relating to age and socio-economic grouping as determinants of the willingness and ability to drive;
- the budget constraint represented by the household's income.

Age and socio-economic factors will play an increasingly important role in shaping automobile demand in the OECD area. Demographic trends in many of the developed countries indicate a fall in the size of households during the 1980s, and a likely increase in the percentage of single-person households. The main implication of a fall in household size is that, by reducing the extent of vehicle-sharing, it provides further scope for growth in car ownership levels and hence demand. The possibility of increases in the amount of leisure time available to households (e.g. as a result of work-sharing, new technology, etc.) and hence an increased desire for mobility, would in theory support this hypothesis.

Table 6.　Labour force participation rates[1]
of females, selected countries

Percentage

	1950	1977
Sweden	35	70
Denmark	50	67
Finland	60	65
Norway	37	59
United Kingdom	41	57
U.S.A.	37	56
Italy	32	37
Ireland	37	33
Spain	18	33
Netherlands	29	32
Greece	42	31

1.　Defined as labour force of all ages divided by population aged 15-64.
Source : OECD, Observer, No. 104, May 1980.

Future trends in labour participation rates will also play a role in determining vehicle ownership levels. The strong rise in female participation rates in some OECD countries since 1950 has partly explained the recent growth of demand for automobiles, since it has both raised household incomes and stimulated the demand for second family cars.

3.　M. Bates and J. Roberts, "Forecasts for the Ownership and Use of a Car", paper presented to *Round Table 55* of ECMT (1981).

B. Levels and growth of income

The size of net or disposable income is a key determinant of automobile demand over the *long term*. However, it has proved difficult to pinpoint the relationship between these variables, since it is not clear which measure of disposable income is relevant to car ownership. In this regard, it is worth noting Parish's contention[4] that household car ownership is to a large degree determined by the household's permanent or expected income, and is unaffected by transitory/windfall income changes. This theory helps explain the continued growth of car ownership during periods of low economic growth.

Various studies have attempted to measure the responsiveness of quantities demanded to changes in income, usually expressed in terms of the income elasticity of demand[5]. For example, in the US, Wykoff estimated income elasticities at around 2.5 in the 1950s and between –0.6 and 2.4 in the late 1960s; Suits and Chows' estimates were approximately 4.0 and 1.8 respectively in the late 1950s. Six studies made in the United States during the 1970s indicate a range in income elasticities between those of Hess (0.26) and Johnson (1.0). The Industries Assistance Commission recently quoted a figure of 1.4 for the Australian market. The Secretariat has made some calculations for other markets which show the following elasticities for 1960-70 and 1975-79 periods respectively: France (2.3, 1.6), Italy (4.1, 3.3), Germany (3.0, 1.6), the United Kingdom (3.0, 1.0), Japan (3.7, 1.4).

The above data indicate a general fall in income elasticities of automobile demand in the last 20 years or so. This could be expected as sales growth tapers off as markets become progressively mature. This observed downward trend in income elasticities obviously needs to be incorporated, and accurately predicted, when income-based forecasting models are used; the failure to do so can lead to serious over-estimation of automobile demand.

C. Operating costs and Vehicle prices

The combined cost of purchasing and operating a vehicle is a major determinant of demand. It may be argued that *operating costs* (especially those costs which are mileage-dependent, e.g. fuel, repairs) have little influence on car ownership, and hence demand, in the short term. Changes in such variable costs mainly result in adjustments in car usage, rather than automobile demand, over the short term. This view is based on the empirically-observed tendency for household transportation budgets to generally remain constant over time[6]: increases in certain expense items are offset by corresponding decreases in other items within the transport budget. (For instance, increases in fuel costs lead to a downward adjustment in distance travelled). If car ownership and demand are affected, it is usually observed over the medium term with a shift down to smaller vehicle sizes.

The way in which adjustments occur within a motorist's transportation budget is shown by the accompanying graph for France; it gives an approximation of the effect of increasing fuel costs on some other automobile expenditure variables. When the real cost of gasoline in France increased markedly in 1974 (shown as an index of the amount

---

4. D. J. Parish, *"car Ownership Forecasting in Category Analysis"*, PTRC July 1975.
5. Defined as the percentage change in quantity demanded resulting from a 1 per cent change in income.
6. For example, Mogridge (1978) found that in the United Kingdom over the period 1971-1975, household expenditure on owning and using a car remained at about 15 per cent of household income. Similarly, the proportion has been consistently around the 12 per cent mark in the United States (see *"Role of the Motor Vehicle in the United States Economy: Quarterly Economic Indicators, Transport Systems Center,"* 30th September, 1980).

Graph 1

FRANCE

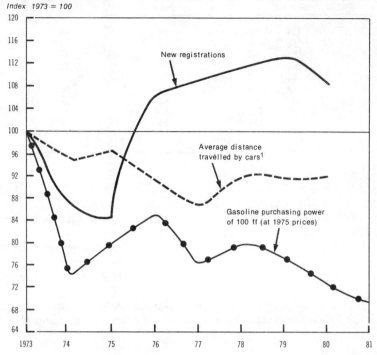

Index 1973 = 100

1. The data refer to recently-purchased vehicles (i.e. within six months prior to the date of each survey).

Sources : Registrations and Annual Kilometrage : Bureau Permanent International des Constructeurs d'automobiles. *Gasoline prices :* derived from data in " L'Argus " (1981 edition).

of gasoline which can be purchased with 100 francs in 1975 prices), the motorists' initial response was both to travel less and to reduce or postpone new vehicle purchases. In following years (post 1975), the continued rise in fuel costs was mainly reflected in further reduction in average distances travelled. Vehicle registrations recovered only after 1975, arguably because motorists could no longer postpone decisions to scrap or trade-in old vehicles. The strength of new car sales beyond this 1975-76 market adjustment period would possibly involve the influence of the income factors rather than the fuel cost or automobile usage factors.

The *fixed cost* component (which incorporates new automobile prices and related costs such as insurance and registration) has a greater influence on automobile demand than do variable costs; fixed costs also influence demand over a shorter time horizon than do variable costs. However price elasticities of automobile demand, which measure the relationship between the purchase price of automobiles and changes in quantity demanded, are very difficult to estimate precisely. As well as arriving at both a reasonable definition and measurement of the actual cost as perceived by the consumer, there is likely to be some delay in these cost effects being reflected in demand.

Such difficulties, together with differences in methodologies adopted (e.g. cross-sectional versus aggregate data), temporal shifts and particular country situations have led to wide variances in estimates of the elasticity of demand for automobiles as a function of their price. For example, we see the following price elasticity estimates for

Table 7.   **Comparison of new vehicle prices (tax inclusive) EEC countries, november 1981**

'000 French francs

Model	Denmark	U.K.	Ireland	France	Neths.	Belgium	F.R.G.	Lux.
Audi 80 GLE	114	84	63	55	60	49	47	41
BMW 320	98	76	77	65	63	54	51	48
Citroën GSA Club	61	48	45	42	39	35	33	31
Fiat 127 Sp.	46	39	38	35	32	27	26	25
Ford Escort 1.3	61	48	–	38	37	33	30	28
VW Golf 1.5	84	59	52	46	47	38	36	33
Volvo 343	72	49	49	42	40	37	37	31
Average	77	58	54	46	45	39	37	34

Source :   Bureau Européen des Unions de Consommateurs ; quoted in *Que Choisir,* Nov. 1981.

the United States: –1.31 (Atkinson 1950), –1.0 (Suits, 1958), –0.1 to –1.8 (Wykoff, 1968) and –0.8 to –2.4 (Carlson, 1976); for the United Kingdom: –1.5 (Department of Industry, 1979) and –1 to –3 (Rhys, 1979); for France: –0.45 (quoted by Feeney and Tanner, 1980); for Australia: –0.3 (IAC, 1980).

The data in Table 7 show the marked differences in consumer prices between EC countries for what are basically identical vehicles. These differences arise mainly from the differences in the levels of taxes imposed on automobiles by the respective governments[7].

The growth in motorisation cannot be explained solely in terms of vehicle prices; but, as Graph 2 shows, new vehicle price levels do, of course, have an impact on new car demand.

Graph 2

RELATIONSHIP BETWEEN NEW VEHICLE PRICES
AND GROWTH IN CAR PARK

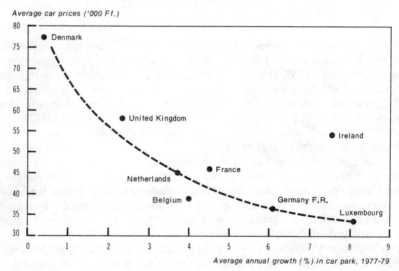

7.   Exchange rate movements explain only a small proportion of these differentials. The data in Graph 2 are based on November 1981 exchange rates; a re-basing of this data in terms of November 1979 exchange rates actually strengthened the correlation between vehicle prices and car park growth.

Table 8, which gives relative pre-tax car prices in various EC countries, is worth considering in terms of industry policy issues. In Denmark at least, manufacturers seem to lower their prices to counterbalance high motoring taxes, i.e. charging only what the market will bear. This contrasts with the United Kingdom where, although the growth of motor car use has been relatively slow in recent years, manufacturers' prices have remained among the highest in the EC – presumably as a result of structural problems within the United Kingdom automobile industry.

One further point of interest is that the three EC countries with the lowest tax-free vehicle prices (Denmark, Luxembourg and the Netherlands) are also those with little or no domestic manufacturing capability. Foreign manufacturers could be using these markets to "top-up" their overall sales, and adopting marginal cost pricing practices to this end.

Table 8.　**Tax-free vehicle prices in EEC countries, as a proportion of U.K. price, november 1981**

Percentages

	Denmark	Luxembourg	Netherlands	Belgium	F.R.G.	France	Ireland	U.K.
Audi 80 GLE	54	55	60	59	63	62	64	100
BMW 320	52	71	69	72	72	79	87	100
Citroën GSA Club	53	73	70	73	77	83	81	100
Fiat 127 Sp.	52	71	69	70	72	83	84	100
Ford Escort 1.3	54	66	65	69	70	73	–	100
VW Golf 1.5	59	64	67	64	67	72	76	100
Volvo 343	60	72	68	75	82	80	84	100
Average	55	67	67	69	72	76	79	100

Source :　Bureau Européen des Unions de Consommateurs, quoted in *Que Choisir*, November 1981.

The cost of credit can also influence new vehicle prices and hence automobile demand. For example, the high interest rates recently prevailing in the United States have contributed to the marked slowdown in the US automobile market. The terms of loan finance (e.g. length of repayment allowed) also may be relevant in some countries, to the extent that they can either moderate or exacerbate any consumer resistance to increases in vehicle prices. Generally speaking, however, the credit factor is mainly relevant over the short-term. Any long-term impact might be traced to institutionalised monetary practices, for example where bank finance for certain "luxury" items such as cars has historically been made restrictive by the central banking authority.

A related effect on new automobile demand is the differential between new and used automobile prices. Some evidence suggests that this differential has widened recently in the United States. While the price of new cars has increased (partly as a result of the incorporation of new technology and safety equipment), the trade-in value of used cars has risen less slowly because of their accelerated technical obsolescence. Thus, the additional cost which must be borne by the consumer in switching to newer models is higher; this may have a detrimental impact on new car sales.

In some instances, on the other hand, differentials between new and used vehicle prices may narrow because of import restrictions. This can happen when the value of used imported cars is maintained at levels significantly higher than would be the case if additional imports of new cars were allowed. A low differential price would be expected to lower the cost of trading-in such vehicles against new domestically-produced vehicles, provided the price of the latter has not increased significantly as a result of industry protection.

Another important effect of higher new vehicle prices (leading to a widening of the new/used price differential) can be to increase the attractiveness of older models. This will affect the rate of depreciation and hence the age at which vehicles are scrapped. The initial result would be a lengthening of the economic lives of used cars, including even large, fuel-inefficient cars, if the cost of switching to new models was high. Sales of new cars, particularly those at the higher end of the price range, would thus be depressed.

D. Geographic factors

In developed markets, car ownership levels tend to be lower in urban than in rural areas because of the transport alternatives to the automobile available in cities (public transport, walking) and the problems of traffic congestion and parking.

The supply and quality of public transport appears to be more important in influencing vehicle ownership than is the level of urbanisation[8]. Thus, all other things being equal, a decline in urban public transport services, such as that which has occurred recently in some European cities, might be expected to extend the growth parameters of automobile ownership, at least in the less heavily-populated urban areas. The trend towards smaller cars, and also the long-term possibilities for an expansion of multi-car ownership through the use of electric commuter vehicles, are also factors which would support this development. Whether improvements in urban public transport, on the other hand, would reduce automobile demand, is a moot point. Scattered evidence suggests that a complementary relationship might exist between public and private transport where improvements in the former lead to a greater general desire to travel.

The movement of people away from inner city areas towards medium-density urban areas may be a long-term source for future growth in car ownership. Such a shift is presently occurring in many OECD countries, although the future trend is difficult to discern. Financial and land-use constraints to the development of road infrastructures could however worsen traffic congestion in new population areas, and place an upper limit on growth in car ownership in the medium and long term.

Outside the OECD area, the effect of population shifts on vehicle ownership may be the reverse of the OECD situation. Only in urban areas are incomes sufficiently high to support vehicle ownership; as the influx of rural workers into cities accelerates, some startling increases in vehicle ownership can be seen. Several of the Latin American cities, especially Mexico City, are examples in this regard.

E. Institutional factors

The post-war development of road infrastructures has been a pre-condition of much of the expansion of automobile use in the OECD area. It is unlikely that a similar growth in road networks will be seen in the next 20 years; much of Northern Europe and North America are now well-served with road systems. Moreover, further marginal improvements over the medium-term are likely to be treated as low priority by governments attempting to curtail aggregate public spending.

The same might be said for much of the non-OECD area (at least the oil-importing countries), where economic difficulties over the short to medium term will restrict the ability to expand road infrastructures. In many non-OECD countries the ongoing lack of suitable roads not only may slow the development of automobile markets, but will tend to ensure that the vehicle characteristics generally demanded in these areas

---

8. Analysis in Britain has shown that areas of good and poor access to public transport may lead to differences in vehicle ownership of up to 60 cars per thousand population.

continue to differ from those in developed markets. OECD manufacturers will have to take greater account of this difference as competition in these markets intensifies.

Societies' demands with respect to environmental control and automobile safety will have a significant impact on the type of vehicle demanded. Whether the actual level of automobile demand is affected to any appreciable extent is difficult to assess; any changes would be mostly reflected through the price elasticity of demand.

Automobile demand beyond the short term can also be influenced by the orientation of transport policy, especially through its impact on the transport modal split (i.e. the respective shares of the total transport task performed by rail, road, sea and air). However, shifting the modal split either towards or away from road transport has often been shown to be rather difficult.

For example, policies aimed at shifting heavy traffic from road to rail (e.g. to reduce traffic congestion and/or provide more space for private automobiles) have, generally speaking, been unsuccessful. Likewise, efforts to shift commuters on to public transport have often been made difficult by the high value which motorists place on transport flexibility and individuality. Moreover, while a number of possibilities are emerging (e.g. car pooling, monorail) which may assist transport planners to reduce dependence on the automobile, it is debatable whether they will influence the evolution of automobile demand to any marked extent. This is not to say that a fundamental shift in transport policy, whereby use of the automobile might be "choked off", could not occur over the long-term. However, this would have serious political and economic implications, given the central role which the automobile has attained in society (at least in the OECD area) as a source of employment, of government revenues and as an integral part of modern-day life.

Summary

The preceding list of demand determinants, while not exhaustive, does highlight the difficulties involved in forecasting saturation levels and, thus, in precisely forecasting automobile demand. Some factors will mainly affect vehicle usage, while others will affect final vehicle demand via a complex decision-making process on the part of the consumer.

Moreover, the decision to own an automobile (or trade-up to a newer model) will often involve non-economic factors. In this regard, there are deep-seated psychological factors at play – the desire for privacy, status, faster travel – which can sustain automobile ownership and demand when economic circumstances would suggest otherwise. It is worth remembering that experience has shown that practically all forecasts have underestimated the further growth of car ownership in industrialised countries and overestimated that in developing countries.

2. LONG-TERM DEMAND SCENARIO

The foregoing discussion highlighted the multitude and complexity of factors determining automobile demand over the long-term. Any attempt to incorporate such variables in an economic model is thus a highly speculative exercise. For this reason, the following Secretariat calculations should be considered as representing broadly indicative scenarios or ranges of magnitude, rather than "official" statistics necessarily agreed to by all Member countries.

The approach adopted by the Secretariat basically assumes that past interrelationships between the many variables (which ultimately determine the number of cars per head of population) hold true in the future. Vehicle densities for each market are thus projected forward by means of a growth function, towards a theoretical saturation level, or asymptote. In other words, a market penetration model of this sort subsumes all the various demand determinants within the projections of vehicle densities.

The second stage involves multiplying these vehicle density projections by the likely population to give estimates of the future car park. Year-on-year changes in the car park are equivalent to new (or first-time) demand. The third stage entails the application of vehicle scrapping rates to the car park estimates, which determines the level of replacement demand. The Annex to this document provides a more complete explanation of the methodology and the various assumptions supporting it, as well as the data calculated by the Secretariat for each of the 39 country/region markets examined.

Main features of the Model's results

Tables 9 and 10 give an overall view of the projected developments in automobile demand by major region[9]. The data suggest that by the year 2000, North America and Western Europe each will account for 29 per cent of World demand (down from 38 per cent and 34 per cent respectively). The shares represented by the other regional markets are expected to increase: Asia (from 14 per cent at present to 19 per cent), Latin America (6 per cent to 12 per cent), Eastern Europe (7 per cent to 8 per cent) and Africa (2 per cent to 3 per cent).

In terms of *annual market growth,* the likely developments beyond 1985 in the various markets may be classified as follows:

- in excess of 5 per cent: The Asian LDCs (excluding India), Brazil, Mexico and Turkey.
- between 3 per cent and 5 per cent: Republic of South Africa, rest of Africa, USSR, rest of Comecon, the balance of Latin America, Spain, Portugal, Greece and India.

Table 9. **World automobile demand, 1979 to 2000**

Million units

	1979[1]	1985	1990	2000
North America	11.6	12.4	12.5	13.4
Latin America	1.8	2.5	3.3	5.4
Western Europe[2]	10.3	11.2	11.8	13.6
Asia[3]	4.4	6.2	7.0	8.7
Africa	0.5	0.8	1.0	1.4
Eastern Europe	2.0	2.1	2.6	3.9
Total	30.5	35.2	38.1	46.6
	Percentage of total			
North America	38	35	33	29
Latin America	6	7	9	12
Western Europe[2]	34	32	31	29
Asia[3]	14	18	18	19
Africa	2	2	3	3
Eastern Europe	7	6	7	8
Total	100	100	100	100

1. 1979 data supplied by Toyota Motor Sales Co. Ltd.
2. Including Yugoslavia.
3. Including OECD Oceania and Middle East.
Note : Figures may not add due to rounding.

9. See the Annex for detailed country projections.

- between 2 per cent and 3 per cent: Yugoslavia.
- between 1 per cent and 2 per cent: Australia, Austria, Belgium, Italy, Finland, Japan, New Zealand, France, Ireland, the Netherlands, Norway, the United States and Switzerland.
- below 1 per cent: Canada, Germany, the United Kingdom, Denmark, Luxembourg and Sweden.

Table 10. **Annual rates of growth in automobile demand, 1970 to 2000**

Annual percentage growth

	Actual 1970-1980	1980-1990	1990-2000
North America	1.1	0.8	0.7
Latin America	n.a.	5.8	5.1
Western Europe[1]	3.2	1.3	1.4
Asia[2]	n.a.	4.3	2.2
Africa	n.a.	6.6	3.5
Eastern Europe	n.a.	2.4	4.2
Total World	2.4	2.0	2.0

1. Including Yugoslavia.
2. Including OECD Oceania and Middle East.

OECD area

The Secretariat projections suggest that a number of OECD markets (including Italy, France, FR Germany, Japan, Spain and, to a lesser extent, the United Kingdom and the Netherlands) are expected to grow less than 2 per cent per year, mainly because these markets are now approaching their mature phase. At that point, replacement demand typically accounts for some 85 per cent or more of total demand, and thus progressively becomes a direct function of the average lifetime of the automobile. This development is not all bad, however, since vehicle scrapping rates in a number of OECD markets are currently below their expected long-term level.

This is because new car sales were relatively buoyant in such markets in the early and late 1970s. These strong sales maintained a vehicle age profile which is younger than would be expected in markets at such stages of maturation. Thus vehicles purchased during these years should be reaching scrapping age by the mid 1980s and early 1990s, and hence boost replacement demand.

Another factor underlying the relatively low scrapping rates in some OECD markets in recent years has been the spread of automobile use. The increased ownership of automobiles by young people, and low-income families as well as the rise of the multi-car household has probably kept old cars on the road longer. With the gradual saturation of such market segments, vehicle scrapping rates should begin to move towards the reciprocal of the average lifetime of the automobile, which typically ranges from around 10 years (e.g. Belgium, France, FR Germany) to 16 years (e.g. Sweden).

New (first-time) automobile demand in the OECD area must obviously weaken, however, in line with the progressive diffusion of the automobile among the population. This expansion is expected to taper-off substantially by around 1990 in most of the more mature markets. By then, new demand will be around 50 per cent lower than current levels. Japan's late but strong growth in automobile use may make it an exception, at least until the mid-1980s, when annual new demand is projected at almost 1.8 million units, or some 600 000 units above the 1979-80 level. On the other hand land-use patterns, and to a lesser extent vehicle operating costs, are expected to significantly brake further expansion of automobile use after 1985.

To summarise the OECD Secretariat's scenario, demand growth in the next two decades is expected to be lower than it was in the 1960s and 1970s (see Table 10). However, the OECD region will continue to be the most important market in absolute terms. Between 1985 and 2000, sizeable expansion is projected, e.g. the United States (additional 880 000 unit sales), Spain (480 000), France (400 000), Italy (340 000), Japan (330 000) and the United Kingdom (190 000).

Non-OECD area

The LDC automobile markets, on the whole, are expected to show significant rates of growth, albeit from rather low bases. The largest increases in absolute market size in the non-OECD area between 1985 and 2000 are likely to be Brazil (1.58 million additional unit sales), USSR (1.16 million), Mexico (760 000), the Middle East (670 000) and the rest of Comecon (590 000).

The main factor sustaining market expansion in the LDC area will be new demand. Replacement demand is likely to remain low during the 1980s, vehicles are kept in the car park as long as technically possible. New vehicle purchases by wealthy motorists will be proximate measures of additions to vehicle stocks, in view of the low vehicle scrapping rates in much of the area. The Middle East is the exception; annual scrapping rates here are currently around 20 per cent due to both weather conditions and the weakness of the second-hand vehicle market. However, as car ownership gathers pace among the middle-income groups, scrapping rates are expected to fall to around 15 per cent.

It should be pointed out that the LDC projections are the most likely to deviate from actual experience, since a high proportion of total demand comes from new purchases. These in turn are more susceptible to the vagaries of economic conditions (beyond the short-term, at least). The projections are, however, on the conservative side compared to estimates made in 1977 by the IFO Institut and the German Vehicle Producers Association (VDA).

Summary and Conclusions

Two interrelated factors are particularly important in assessing the future demand for automobiles: vehicle lifetime and scrapping rates. Historical developments in many countries indicate a progressive increase in average vehicle lifetime. Also replacement demand and scrapping rates tend to increase as market saturation increases and the vehicle stock gradually ages. The Secretariat projections assume that no significant changes will occur in government policies which could influence these factors. It should not, however, be overlooked that vehicle lifetime for instance could be influenced by governments' approaches to testing and registration procedures, speed limits, taxation, safety or environmental concerns, etc.

In summary, the OECD Secretariat's projections are that world demand for automobiles by 1990 could be 25 per cent higher than at present, with only a slightly smaller increase (22 per cent) between 1990 and the year 2000. The difficulties recently experienced in most countries could however change the future perspectives[10]. As the data in Table 11 suggest, much of the market growth during the course of the 1980s will stem from increased replacement demand, and this component is expected to rise from

---

10. Table 12 provides a comparison between the OECD Secretariat estimate of future demand and those from other agencies.

Table 11. **Replacement demand as share of total demand,
by region, 1980 to 2000**

Percentage

	1980	1990	2000
North America	67	82	87
EEC	68	82	87
Scandinavia	71	82	85
Other Europe	24	61	74
OECD - Pacific	64	78	84
Total OECD	66	80	86
Comecon	25	42	57
Africa	50	52	57
Latin America	27	37	50
Asia	40	50	56
Total non OECD	30	43	56
Total world	58	71	76

58 per cent to 71 per cent of total demand by 1990. The continued market expansion projected in the 1990s will also result chiefly from the replacement component; although its share of total demand will rise less rapidly than in the 1980s (from 71 per cent to 76 per cent), the growth in vehicle stocks will raise the absolute level of replacement demand by a considerably larger amount.

The foregoing analysis assumes that no major changes in the concept of the automobile which might otherwise have pushed vehicle ownership levels outside the historical growth trend will occur over the next 10 years. The projections also assume that the inter-relationships between various demand variables will remain approximately the same.

The main impact of the LDC growth scenario, in terms of world automobile demand, may not be seen until the 1990s. However, scrapping rates and hence replacement demand in many of the developed markets will be rising in the intervening period. This should enable world automobile demand in the 1980s to match the projection of 2.0 per cent annual growth for the 1990s.

Table 12. **Comparison of Secretariat's demand projections (medium variant)
with those of other agencies**
Million units

Agency (and date of compilation)	1985	1990	2000
USA			
Arthur Anderson & Co. (1980)	11.5	12.8	–
US Dept. of Transportn. (1980)	11.6	11.2	–
Sec. OECD (1981)	11.3	11.5	12.2
A.D. Little Inc. (1980)	–	–	12.3e
DRI (1981)	10.4 (1986)	–	–
Int'l Business Reports (1980)	10.4	–	–
Western Europe			
IFO - Interfutures (1977)	14.4	14.8	–
VDA - Interfutures (1977)	13.4	14.1	14.9
Eurofinance (1980)	12.4	–	–
Toyota (1981)	–	–	–
A.D. Little Inc. (1980)	–	12.6	–
Economist Intell. Unit (1980)	11.3	–	–
Sec. OECD (1981)	11.2	11.9	13.6
DRI (1981)	11.0 (1986)	–	–
Japan			
RIIM (1981)	5.4	5.9	–
IFO - Interfutures (1977)	4.6	4.1	–
A.D. Little Inc. (1980)	–	–	4.3
Sec. OECD (1981)	4.4	4.3	4.7
DRI (1981)	3.2 (1986)	–	–
TOTAL OECD			
IFO - Interfutures (1977)	34.4	36.5	–
Sec. OECD	28.6	29.3	32.6
Eurofinance (1980)	28.0	29.0	–
DRI (1981)	25.6e (1986)	–	–
Eastern Europe			
A.D. Little Inc. (1980)	–	–	5.1e
IFO - Interfutures (1977)	2.9	3.9	–
Toyota (1981)	–	3.9	–
Sec. OECD (1981)	2.1	2.6	3.9
Africa			
IFO - Interfutures (1977)	0.9	1.2	–
Sec. OECD (1981)	0.8	1.0	1.4
Toyota (1981)	–	0.9	–
A.D. Little Inc. (1980)	–	–	1.1
Latin America			
IFO - Interfutures (1977)	3.4	4.9	–
Sec. OECD (1981)	2.5	3.3	5.4
Toyota (1981)	–	2.8	–
A.D. Little Inc. (1980)	–	–	4.5e
Asia (incl. Japon, Aust., N.Z.)			
Toyota (1981)	–	6.8	–
Sec. OECD (1981)	6.5	7.0	8.7
Total world			
IFO - Interfuturs (1977)	42.5	48.0	–
Eurofinance (1980)	38.0	43.0	–
Toyota (1981)	–	40.8	–
A.D. Little Inc. (1980)	–	–	47.9
Sec. OECD (1981)	35.4	38.1	46.4
DRI (1981)	33.4 (1986)	–	–

Note : DRI = Data Resources International, London ; IFO = IFO Institut, Köln ; VDA = Verband der Automobilindustrie, Frankfurt ; RIIM = Research Institute of Industrial Materials, Japan.

Table 13. Estimates of passenger automobile stocks

Millions units

	1980 actual	1990					2000
		VDA	IFO	Toyota	Average	OECD	OECD
North America	134	140	145	159	148	148	168
Western Europe	108	126	143	136	135	135	158
Oceania	31	41	50	n.a.	46	49	57
Total OECD	273	307	337	n.a.	322	329	383
Eastern Europe	17[2]	31	34	32	32	29	46
Latin America	20[2]	29	39	36	35	36	57
Asia[1]	8	19	12	n.a.	16	15	27
Africa	6	12	10	10	11	10	16
Total Non-OECD[1]	51	91	95	n.a.	93	90	146
Total World[1]	324	398	432	434	421	419	529

1. Excluding China and North Korea.
2. Estimation.

Table 14. Estimates of passenger automobile densities

Vehicles per '000 population

	1980 actual	1990		2000	
		OECD	IFO-Institut	OECD	VDA
North America	532	547	530	580	500
Western Europe	259	307	315	339	308
Japan	202	323	320	360	280
Australia, New Zealand	390	452	500	482	460
Total OECD	340	389	385	422	372
Eastern Europe	45	71	85	106	176
Latin America	49	75	85	99	100
Asia[1]	5	8	7	12	n.a.
Africa	13	16	17	19	26
Total Non-OECD[1]	19	27	30	36	n.a.
Total World[1]	93	100	107	106	n.a.

1. Excluding China and North Korea.

Annex

METHODOLOGY AND ASSUMPTIONS
UNDERLYING THE SECRETARIAT'S LONG-TERM
AUTOMOBILE DEMAND PROJECTIONS

The discussion of automobile demand determinants in the main document highlights some of the problems involved in measuring and ranking various demand influences. The incorporation of economic variables in a forecasting model can also become a very speculative exercise if the future path of personal incomes, vehicle prices, petrol prices, etc, are an integral part of such an exercise. Forecasts of such variables beyond the short term vary widely between agencies, and are perhaps little better than educated guesses[1].

The Secretariat has not attempted to model directly the various determinants of automobile demand. Instead, the technique used basically extrapolates historical relationships towards a long-term asymptote or level of market saturation. This technique could undoubtedly be improved upon in certain country situations where reliable data allow for more sophisticated techniques to be engaged; however, the importance of having a standard method across all countries so as to allow a comparison and evaluation of underlying assumptions made was a major factor in favour the more straightforward approach decided upon. The results of the projections are the Secretariat's responsibility and are not necessarily agreed upon or endorsed by Member countries.

Method of projection

The method adopted by the Secretariat involves three separate steps:

a) use of a logistic growth function to project car ownership levels (i.e. the number of vehicles per thousand population)
b) multiplying these ratios by population estimates to arrive at likely vehicle stocks (car parks)
c) applying scrapping rates to the car park of each country/region, so as to derive replacement demand. (New demand equals the year-on-year change in the car park.)

These stages are briefly described below:

i) Estimating car ownership

Automobile markets conform rather well to the theory of market penetration and the corresponding concept of saturation. That is, automobile markets move over time towards respective levels of saturation, a final stage where every person who chooses to or can own a car does, in fact, do so.

While the market penetration path can be specified by rather sophisticated algebraic formulae which build in income and other variables, a simple function is used here, namely:

$$ln\ P_T = a - \frac{b}{T^c}$$

where ln = normal log
P_T = number of passenger cars per thousand people in year T.
a = saturation level, *b* and *c* are coefficients
ln P_T approaches over time to saturation value *a*.

A characteristic of this function is the assumption that, over time, the level of car ownership initially increases slowly from a low base, and then enters a period of more rapid growth. As ownership becomes widespread, a slowdown occurs in the absolute size of the annual increase in car ownership. The model

---

1. The OECD no longer prepares medium-term or long-term GDP forecasts.

28

therefore rests on the hypothesis that, over time, the level of car ownership follows an S-shaped curve (non-symmetrical in this case) which eventually reaches a saturation level at which no further growth occurs[2].

The model determines future car ownership largely on the basis of past relationships – no direct allowance is made for changes in incomes and prices[3]. The projected values of car ownership also depends however on an estimate of the saturation level. Such an estimate, which can only be subjectively determined, is time-indefinite; it represents a future reference point to which the logistic curve gravitates.

The Secretariat's saturation estimates (see Table 1) are underpinned by the fact that roughly 60 per cent to 63 per cent of each country's population is legally and physically able to drive a car. In terms of potential car ownership, this means a maximum saturation level of 600-630 passenger cars per thousand people if the possibility of multi-car ownership is excluded. For most countries, such a level is unlikely. While there is already some evidence of multi-car ownership (e.g. USA, some Arab oil states), it would need to be very substantial if a saturation level of 600 was to be reached, since it would need to counter-balance the likelihood that not all those between 17 and 70 years will, in practice, own their own car[4].

The saturation estimates were derived by firstly ranking the OECD countries in terms of

i) present vehicle densities,
ii) present income per capita and
iii) current population densities per square kilometre.

Table 1. **Estimated saturation levels (asymptotes) of automobile markets**

700	USA	430	Greece
650	Canada	400	Denmark
600	Switzerland		Turkey
	Luxembourg	350	Portugal
550	France		Yugoslavia
	F.R. Germany		Argentina
	Australia		Brazil
	New Zealand		Mexico
	Iceland		Middle East
520	Austria		USSR
	Belgium		Other Comecon
500	Italy		Republic of South
	Netherlands		Africa
480	Sweden	200	ASEAN
450	UK		Rest of South America
	Japan (initially 610*)		Rest of Central
	Spain (initially 530*)		America
	Norway		South East Asia
	Ireland		(excl. ASEAN)
440	Finland	100	India
			Middle South Asia
			Rest of Africa

* See country notes.
Note : The above figures relate to *theoretical* saturation levels, and do not necessarily reflect an opinion of the likely actual saturation level to be reached many years hence. For example, India's saturation level could well by 500 or 600, income growth permitting. Strictly speaking « asymptote » better describes the situation.

2. For a more detailed discussion see *Development of Methods for Forecasting Car Ownership and Use*, G.E. Giles and T.E. Worsley, U.K. Department of Transport, and *Methods of Forecasting Car Ownership* in *Car Ownership and Use*, Programme for Road Research OECD 1982.

3. However the methodology used does incorporate various demand determinants in three indirect ways:

− since the projections are essentially based on historical trends (and that the influence of various factors is subsumed under these historical trends), they implicitly assume that the aggregate effect of the various influences will continue to be the same as previously e.g. a fall in incomes would be offset by perhaps a corresponding fall in vehicle prices or in miles travelled.
− each country's saturation level as estimated (see Table 4) incorporates implicit judgements as to the following sorts of factors: incomes, population structure, vehicle and fuel prices, geographical land forms (and population densities), general attitudes to car ownership, etc.
− each country's future vehicle scrapping rates as estimated (see *(iii)* below) reflect implicit judgements as to factors such as car quality, climate, new and second-hand vehicle prices, fuel prices, etc.

4. For example, it is unlikely that *(i)* all families of two parents and two children of say ages 17-19 would own four cars and *(ii)* that retired couples of 60-65 years of age would require two cars.

These rankings were separately weighted in reference to a "leader" country and the three weights were aggregated to give a final ranking. A saturation level for the top-ranking country, the United States was then set at 700[5] and the remaining countries were given saturation levels broadly in proportion to their weight vis-a-vis the United States weight.

These saturation estimates were subsequently adjusted slightly on the basis of comments by Secretariat staff from the countries concerned: some minor adjustments were also made following the comparison of historical data and the model's predicted values. Manipulation of this sort was considered necessary in view of the sensitivity of the estimates of the more developed markets to different saturation levels. The saturation estimates for non-OECD countries were generally set at the lower end of the OECD table; demand estimates for these countries were found to be relatively insensitive to the saturation levels used.

ii) Population projections

The second step involved the saturation-derived vehicle densities for each country/region (1985, 1990 and 2000) being multiplied by U.N. population projections[6] to give estimates of the car park.

Since the population data was mainly assembled in 1976-1977, some discrepancies have already been found between the UN 1980 estimates and the actual 1980 data. In such cases, the high or low population variants were substituted.

iii) Application of vehicle scrapping rates

The third step involves the application of scrapping rates to the various car park data. This gives replacement demand, while the year-on-year change in the projected car park represents new demand.

The scrapping rate is defined as the proportion of the vehicle stock which is scrapped, or in other words, ceases to exist as far as vehicle registration statistics are concerned. That is, it covers vehicles no longer registrable due to wear and tear, accident "write-offs", exports of second-hand vehicles, etc.

The estimation of future scrapping rates is both the most crucial and most difficult aspect of this type of analysis. This is particularly the case in most developed markets where replacement demand (which directly depends on the scrapping rate) is currently about 80 per cent of total demand.

Two quite distinct elements influence a country's scrapping rate. The first is the stage of motorism reached by the country concerned. In the early stages, recently-purchased automobiles form a relatively large proportion of the vehicle stock, and as a result the demand for vehicles to replace scrappings is low. With the gradual ageing of the vehicle stock and as market saturation is neared, replacement demand, and the scrapping rate, increases.

The final stage involves complete saturation where replacement accounts for all sales (except a small amount of new demand arising from any population growth). At this stage, scrapping rates should be roughly in line with the average life of vehicles in the car park. That is, if the average life is 12 years, the annual scrapping rate should in theory be equal to its reciprocal, namely 8.3 per cent.

With respect to the above, the essential problem is in knowing whereabouts on the vehicle density curve a certain country market will be at a certain future date[7]. The market saturation level will be the major determining factor in this regard, along with the approach path followed by the market.

The second, and more important, determinant of scrapping rates is the average lifetime of the automobile. Table 2 shows that, in Sweden at least, there has been a consistent increase in the average lifetimes of passenger cars since 1965. By 1980, Swedish cars were estimated to have a 65 per cent longer life than those in 1965. Although the data for the U.S.A. refers to the average age of the vehicle stock, the increase over time is also indicative of a lengthening vehicle lifetime since 1970. Similar trends are expected in Japan, with the average vehicle lifetime increasing from 8.4 to 10.6 years over the decade to 1990.

Since replacement demand is a direct function of the "longevity" of cars, future increases or decreases in automobile lifetimes will fundamentally influence aggregate demand estimates. Indeed, taking France as an example, the average lifetime appears to be around 10-11 years at present. If this was assumed to increase to 12.5 years by 1990, an annual scrapping rate of about 8.0 per cent would apply, giving replacement demand at 1.7 million vehicles. On the other hand, if the average lifetime was assumed to fall to say 9 years, this would be consistent with the scrapping rate of roughly 11.1 per cent and replacement demand of 2.41 million.

Clearly, therefore, a good deal of attention needs to be given to the likely future trend in the average lifetime of automobiles. A study recently published by the German Motor Vehicle Manufacturers' Association (VDA) considered that, on balance, a continuous increase in the average lifetime may be more likely[8]. The study cited the following arguments for and against such a development:

---

5. The 1979 vehicle density in the United States was 542 and still rising.
6. *World Population Trends and Prospects by Country, 1950-2000*, United Nations, New York, 1979.
7. The utilisation of vehicle suvival curves largely overcomes this problem. However, the detailed data pertaining to various countries' car parks (age, quality, etc.) precluded this.
8. *Trends and Prospects of Average Lifetimes of Passenger Cars* by M.R. Hild (IFC) published in VDA series.

Table 2. **Sweden :**

Median life (years) for passenger cars of certain car makes,
calculated from the scrapping frequencies for the years 1965, 1971 and 1975-1980

Car make	1965	1971	1975	1976	1977	1978	1979	1980
Total average	9.4	12.4	13.9	13.4	14.1	14.4	15.0	15.5
Audi/DKW	8.3	9.9	11.9	11.6	12.0	12.4	12.6	12.5
BMC	8.6	10.2	11.9	11.3	12.1	12.3	13.1	13.5
BMW	9.1	10.5	12.8	12.7	13.3	13.5	14.0	14.4
Citroën	7.8	10.2	12.5	12.7	13.9	13.8	13.6	14.1
Fiat	8.3	10.6	11.7	11.0	11.0	11.4	11.6	11.9
Ford	8.4	11.2	12.7	12.3	12.6	12.9	13.3	13.6
Mercedes-Benz	10.2	12.4	24.7	14.8	15.5	15.2	16.0	16.6
Opel	8.8	11.4	13.1	12.6	13.0	13.5	14.0	14.4
Peugeot	8.6	11.8	12.8	11.8	11.6	11.6	11.7	11.8
Renault	6.9	10.3	12.4	11.9	12.3	12.4	12.6	12.6
SAAB	9.0	11.6	12.2	12.0	12.5	13.1	13.6	14.2
Simca	7.3	9.9	11.6	11.1	11.2	12.2	12.0	12.1
Vauxhall	7.5	10.8	11.9	11.3	11.5	11.9	12.0	12.4
Volkswagen	10.6	13.2	14.2	13.8	14.0	14.3	14.9	15.4
Volvo	10.7	14.2	16.5	16.7	17.5	17.9	18.7	19.3

Source :   AB Svensk Bilprovning (27.8.81).

**Average age of passenger cars
in use in U.S.**

Year	Years old	Year	Years old
1980	6.6	1963	6.0
1979	6.4	1962	6.0
1978	6.3	1961	6.0
1977	6.2	1960	5.9
1976	6.2	1959	5.8
1975	6.0	1958	5.6
1974	5.7	1957	5.5
1973	5.7	1956	5.6
1972	5.7	1955	5.9
1971	5.7	1954	6.2
1970	5.5	1953	6.5
1969	5.5	1952	6.8
1968	5.6	1950	7.8
1967	5.6	1948	8.8
1966	5.7	1946	9.0
1965	5.9	1944	7.3
1964	6.0	1941	5.5

Source :   Estimated by the Motor Vehicle Manufacturers Association of the U.S. Inc.

Arguments for an increase in average lifetime

- Increase of the technical lifetime of the car, e.g. by using more solid materials, rust protection of the undercarriage, etc.;
- Decline of average annual usage of cars (e.g. the shift towards two-car families should result in less kilometrage, and hence less wear and tear per vehicle; rising fuel prices would also induce the same effect);
- Tendency to purchase more sophisticated cars;
- Extension of the demand potential for older cars (youngsters, second car owners, etc.);
- Decline of accident frequency.

Arguments for a decrease in average lifetime

- Demand for more safety;
- More restrictive car inspection regulations;
- Increase of costs for car repair and maintenance;
- Advanced technology, fuel consumption, fashion and comfort of new cars, etc.

The demand projections contained in this chapter tentatively assume that the average life of automobiles in the OECD area will increase over the next two decades. The underlying rationale is similar to that of the VDA. Moreover, historical developments in Sweden and the United States[9] also indicate a progressive increase in either average vehicle lifetimes or the average age of vehicle populations[10].

Outside the OECD area the above arguments are not strictly applicable. There are some plausible reasons (as well as considerable evidence) to suggest that scrapping rates in developing countries will be lower than in developed countries[11]:

a) the lower cost of labour incurred in repairing cars in the LDC's (assuming no marked differences in spare parts prices).

b) motorists in the LDC's are mostly interested in obtaining basic transportation services from a car; the value of older cars is therefore maintained despite the availability of technological/luxury features in newer models.

c) the increasing cost of labour relative to capital in developed economies has led to greater use of production technology (e.g. greater strength, low maintenance materials, etc.), with the result that new vehicle prices have risen in proportion to maintenance and repair costs. This tends to depress the market value of used cars. In the LDC's, on the other hand, the value of older cars is depressed less rapidly by the introduction of new models. That is to say, sales of "new technology" vehicles will be inhibited because of their high initial cost and also because the repair-savings are less significant.

d) the cost of suffering breakdowns is lower in developing countries, because of the lower opportunity cost of labour and time. Thus, although the greater usage of used cars in LDC's increases the possibility of breakdowns and accidents, the motorists discount the value of such cars by much less than would their counterparts in developed countries.

A tentative conclusion to be drawn from these factors is that the average lifetimes of vehicles in LDC countries will not be influenced to the same extent by technological/economic factors as they will in the OECD area. In other words, the average lifetime of vehicles in the LDC area will probably not increase, since they are already at their maximum. Nevertheless, scrapping rates will rise over time in such countries due to the evolution of the car park.

On the basis of the various considerations outlined above, the Secretariat adopted the following procedure to estimate future scrapping rates:

i) deriving historical annual scrapping rates for each country market on the basis of the following identity:
New Registrations = Vehicle Scrappings ± Changes in Vehicle Stock

ii) Expressing the number of vehicle scrappings in each year as a percentage of the vehicle stock at the end of the previous year.

iii) Compiling average annual rates for each of the 1960s and 1970s.

iv) Making judgements of likely trends in the 1980s and 1990s, on the basis of these historical values and the factors described in paragraphs 61-64.

With regard to step *(iii)*, scrapping rates in the 1970s were found to be higher than those for the 1960s in almost all countries. The one exception is Sweden where the scrapping rate fell from 6.7 per cent in the 1960s to 6.6 per cent in the 1970s. This may be partly due to the introduction of stringent vehicle registration procedures in the 1970s, whereby mandatory maintenance and repairs possibly lengthened the service life of vehicles. The advances which Swedish manufacturers have made in building longer-lasting vehicles might also be relevant in this regard.

In the other developed markets, the 1970s scrapping rates were generally 50-100 per cent above those for the 1960s. This is mainly explained by the high growth in motorism during the 1960s, which resulted in the average age of the vehicle stock being low. The same influence also partly accounts for the low scrapping rates in some non-OECD markets at the present time; although the factors outlined in paragraph 63 have arguably had a greater influence.

Step *(iv)* above involved a necessary degree of arbitrariness. This arose in the following ways:

– Simple extrapolation of annual scrapping rates over time was used in some cases, but the difficulty is in knowing at what time an upward sloping trend will level out. Where extrapolation was used, an upper limit was set in line with the estimated present average life of vehicles in the country concerned.

– In cases where vehicle scrapping rates in the 1970s were already at possibly peak rates (e.g. Sweden) the same rates were assumed to continue over the next two decades.

9. The only countries for which the Secretariat has data at present.
10. The average age of the vehicle population is, however, only a proxy for the average lifetime. This is mainly because the average age can sometimes be unduly influenced by the impact of earlier demand fluctuations.
11. See H.G. Grubel *International Trade in Used Cars and Problems of Economic Development*, in *World Development*, Vol. 8 (1980).

–   Another category of country treatment involved the assumption of constant scrapping rates over the long term, but with a temporary increase around 1985 to reflect likely market adjustment. The United States and Canada were treated in this way to reflect the continuing shift to more compact, fuel-efficient vehicles.
–   Scrapping rates in some other countries (e.g. Norway, Finland, New Zealand), were assumed to align with those of nearby, similar markets. This approach was adopted where, in the countries concerned, similar historical growth profiles to those earlier experienced by comparable, further advanced markets were observed. Sweden represents the bench-mark country for Scandinavia, while Australia is likewise in relation to New Zealand[12].

RESULTS OF THE PROJECTIONS

Before describing the main results of the country projections, some brief explanatory comments are necessary to avoid possible misinterpretation.

–   the demand projections, in that they are based on a long-term growth path, are essentially estimates around which cyclical trends will fluctuate.
–   the exercise aims at building up to aggregated regional and world totals. The individual country scenarios are chiefly intended to illustrate the ways in which the main variables might be expected to move in the future, given the relevant data available.
–   Since the model is projecting forward 20 years, historical data back to the 1950s is used wherever possible. As a result, in some markets where strong growth in vehicle ownership has recently occurred (France, the Federal Republic of Germany, Canada, Switzerland, Luxembourg), present vehicle ownership is above the projected level. To overcome this problem requires (a) a substantially higher saturation level, or (b) extrapolation from a considerably shorter historical base. These options were not chosen.
–   the 1985 projections, particularly for the above five countries, should be treated with caution; they have been provided mainly to enable a comparison with other agencies' projections, the majority of which do not extend beyond 1985 on a disaggregated basis.
–   the word "demand" is used interchangeably with "sales", and both terms refer to purchases of new passenger vehicles.
–   "new demand" relates to demand from first-time purchasers (i.e. new entrants to the market), and "replacement demand" represents demand for new cars to replace scrapped vehicles.
–   replacement demand equals the scrapping rate multiplied by the vehicle stock at the end of the previous year.
–   "vehicle density" refers to the number of passenger automobiles per thousand people.

North America

Annual automobile sales in the *United States* are expected to be in the vicinity of 11.3 million units in 1985, or 600 000 units above the 1977-79 average. This is contingent on the scrapping rate rising to 7.5 per cent in 1985 (from the 1970s average of 7.2 per cent) as a result of continuing market adjustment to fuel efficient vehicles. The presently flat market and the associated low rate of scrapping can also be expected to lead to above average scrapping rates around 1983-1985.

Beyond 1985, the market is likely to grow at 0.5 per cent per annum. The main factors involved will be ongoing rises in vehicle densities (though by progressively smaller increments) as well as continuing population growth which will maintain new (first-time) demand at a level in excess of 1.5 million vehicles. The assumption that post-1985 scrapping rates will be below the 1985 level attempts to account for *(a)* the possibility of an increase in average vehicle lifetime and *(b)* the likelihood that most of the larger, fuel-inefficient vehicles will have been already scrapped by this time.

By the 1990s, annual demand is projected to be around 11.5-12.2 million units. As at the year 2000, the vehicle stock will approach 154 million, giving a density of 590 vehicles per thousand population. Replacement demand is expected to represent around 87 per cent of total demand.

In *Canada,* automobile sales in 1985 are expected to be around 1978/79 levels, that is about 1 million units. This estimate implicitly assumes that the high growth in Canada's vehicle density during the late 1970s was a short-term development (perhaps cyclically-based); a slowdown in the growth of the vehicle stock is thus assumed to occur over the medium term[13]. This estimate is also contingent on a small rise in scrapping rates to account for the demand shift away from large, fuel-inefficient vehicles.

---

12.   The New Zealand case is rather special in that, although it is a mature market and has a vehicle density similar to Australia, its average annual scrapping rate has been very low (2.4 per cent in the 1960s, 3.4 per cent in the 1970s). The major explanation for this possibly lies with the operation of import licensing in New Zealand during much of the post-war period. These restrictions have recently been eased.
13.   In 1979 the actual vehicle density of 433 was substantially above the trend value of 391. The vehicle density during the 1990s is thus assumed to grow more slowly so as to enable equilibration with the predicted density of 453 in 1990.

Secretariat estimates of car density
car park and total demand
North America - 1985-2000

Year End December	Car density	Popln	Car park	Demand		
				new	Replacement	total
	Cars '000 people	Million	Million	'000	'000	'000
UNITED STATES						
1979 actual	542.2	222.2	120.5	3 338	6 997	10 335
1980 actual	541.7	222.2	123.5	2 982	5 779	8 761
1985	538.1	232.9	125.3	2 150	9 239	11 338
1990	558.3	243.5	135.9	2 090	9 370	11 460
1995	575.3	252.8	145.4	1 953	10 044	11 997
2000	589.7	260.4	153.6	1 584	10 638	12 220

Assumptions : Saturation : 700 ; Scrapping Rate : 1985 rate to be 7.5 % (compared with 1970s average of 7.2 %). To fall back to 7.0 % from 1990 onwards.

CANADA						
1979 actual	432.6	23.91	10 226	146	692	1 003
1980 actual	n.a.	24.1	n.a.	n.a.	n.a.	932
1985 *	443.6	25.63	11 369	174	840	1 014
1990	452.8	26.95	12 203	166	843	1 009
1995	474.2	28.10	13 325	221	917	1 138
2000	492.7	29.13	14 352	201	991	1 192

Assumptions : Saturation : 650 ; Scrapping Rate : 1985 rate to be 7.5 % (compared with long-term average of 6.3 %). To fall back to 7.0 % from 1990 onwards.

* Adjusted to account for the fact that 1978-79 vehicle densities are significantly above the trend, i.e. 1985 car density is approximately mid-way between 1979 actual and 1990 trend value [$Y_{85} = Y_{79} + 5/11 (Y_{90} - Y_{79})$].

Scrapping rates after 1985 are expected to fall slightly for the same reasons as the US case. Beyond 1985, a market growth of around 1.1 per cent per annum is considered likely, resulting in an annual market of 1.22 million units, and a car park of 14.35 million units, by the year 2000.

EEC Countries

Automobile demand in the *United Kingdom* is projected at around 1.6 million units by 1985, which is slightly below the cyclical peak of 1979.

During the period 1985-2000, sales volume is expected to build up to 1.83 million units, indicating a market growth of 0.7 per cent per year. This compares with an annual growth rate of 3.9 per cent in the 1970s. The main factors underlying this marked slowdown will be the successively smaller additions to the vehicle stock as saturation is approached, minimal population growth, and a levelling of earlier rises in scrapping rates.

With regard to scrapping rates, however, it should be noted that the 1985 rate (8.0 per cent) has been set slightly above the 1970s average (7.8 per cent); this adjustment is based on a trend extrapolation of the continual upward movement in United Kingdom scrapping rates since the mid-1970s. In the post-1985 period, scrapping rates are assumed to remain at around 8.0 per cent, which is consistent with a likely vehicle lifetime of about 12.5 years.

By the year 2000, the total vehicle stock will probably have risen to around 20.7 million units, giving a vehicle density of 365. By this stage, it is expected that replacement demand will account for 90 per cent of sales.

In *France* the 1979 vehicle density (and sales) is considerably above the Secretariat estimated long-term trend, the former being consistent with an eventual saturation of the order of 600. With a saturation level of 550 as estimated by the Secretariat, and assuming a gradual realignment between actual and trend values during the 1990s, sales by 1985 should be around 2.1 million units.

From 1985 onwards, the market is projected to grow by 1.2 per cent per year, resulting in annual sales of 2.2 million by 1990 and rising to almost 2.5 million by the year 2000. By this time, it is expected that replacement demand will constitute 85 per cent of sales and that the vehicle stock will be approximately 25.8 million units.

These estimates for France assume a rise in the annual scrapping rate from 7.3 per cent (1970s' average) to 8.3 per cent by 1985. This does not presuppose a decrease in vehicle lifetimes; rather it attempts to account for the possibility that the 1970s' scrapping rates (as measured) were "artificially" lowered by the strong recent growth in the car park[14]. A rate of 8.3 per cent is consistent with an average vehicle lifetime of about 12.1 years in a saturated market; since the present average vehicle lifetime is thought to be around 10.5 years, this implies a moderate increase in the future.

In the *Federal Republic of Germany*, sales are projected at around 2.3 million by 1985, which is some 300 000 units below the cyclical peak of 1978-1979.

Over the period 1985-2000, market growth is projected to be low (about 0.5 per cent per year); the main factors here could be a decrease in new demand due to saturation being approached as well as a fall in the population. By the year 2000, passenger vehicle stocks could total about 28.4 million, and replacement could account for 90 per cent of sales.

These estimates assume that the scrapping rate will rise from the 1970s' average of 7.0 per cent to around 8.0 per cent by 1985 and thereafter. This is broadly in line with the French scenario. A scrapping rate of 8.0 per cent in 1985 is equivalent to an average vehicle lifetime of about 12.5 years (which is well above the present average vehicle lifetime in the Federal Republic of Germany which is around 10 years).

In *Italy*, 1985 sales are projected at 1.53 million which, although only equivalent to the 1980 level, are some 25-30 per cent above the average annual sales in 1975-1979.

Between 1985 and 1995, annual sales growth is estimated at 1.9 per cent, levelling off thereafter. The main factors underlying the relatively high growth over 1985-1995 could be population increases and a significant rise in scrapping rates. The present rate (4.0 per cent) which is very low by European standards, is probably due to the Italians' tendency to keep small cars for long periods for commuter use. There is also the likelihood that the 1970s' scrapping rates are under-estimates (for the same reasons as in France).

Secretariat estimates of car density car park and total demand

EEC, TEN - 1985-2000

Year End December	Car density	Popln.	Car park	Demand		
				New	Replacement	total
	Cars '000 people	million	'000	'000	'000	'000
UNITED KINGDOM						
1979 actual	268.4	55.95	15 019	602	1 114	1 716
1980 actual	275.9	55.95	15 437	418	1 097	1 515
1985	308.2	55.76	17 185	287	1 352	1 639
1990	331.3	55.85	18 513	257	1 461	1 718
1995	350.2	56.26	19 702	228	1 558	1 786
2000	365.8	56.67	20 730	186	1 643	1 829

Assumptions : Saturation : 450 ; Scrapping Rate : to rise from 1970s average of 7.8 % to 8.0 % by 1985, and thereafter remain constant.

FRANCE						
1979 actual	345.6	53.60	18 440	720	1 256	1 976
1980 actual	356.2	53.70	19 130	690	1 183	1 873
1985	366.8	54.67	20 053	438	1 628	2 066
1990	396.0	55.82	22 105	395	1 802	2 197
1995	420.0	57.07	23 969	363	1 959	2 322
2000	440.1	58.55	25 768	359	2 109	2 468

Assumptions : Saturation : 550 ; Scrapping Rate : to rise from 1970s average of 7.3 % to 8.3 % by 1985 and thereafter remain constant.

GERMANY						
1979 actual	367.9	61.46	22 614	994	1 629	2 623
1980 actual	377.2	61.60	23 236	622	1 804	2 426
1985	398.3	60.01	23 902	468	1 875	2 434
1990	431.8	59.41	25 653	322	2 026	2 348
1995	457.4	59.28	27 115	278	2 147	2 425
2000	477.1	59.55	28 411	252	2 253	2 505

Assumptions : Saturation : 550 ; Scrapping Rate : to rise from 1970s average of 7.0 % to 8.0 % by 1985 and thereafter remain constant.

---

14. That is, in terms of the scrapping rate equation, the denominator (present car park) has increased above its proportional relationship to the numerator (vehicles now being scrapped but purchased 10 or 12 years earlier).

During the 1980s, scrapping rates are assumed to move towards, but not reach, the levels of the United Kingdom, the Federal Republic of Germany and France, stabilizing at 6.0 per cent. This is equivalent to an average vehicle life of 16.6 years.

By the year 2000, the car park is estimated at 26.5 million vehicles, giving a density of 434 vehicles per thousand people – approximately the same as for France. Replacement purchases will account for 85 per cent of total sales by this time.

Automobile sales in *Denmark* are currently well below historical levels and have led to a fall in the vehicle density in 1980. The expensiveness of new vehicles combined with high vehicle operating costs (fuel, registration, etc.) appear to be important in this regard.

The opinion has thus been expressed[15] that motorism in Denmark is now almost at its saturation level. While such a view is probably valid in a short-term context, the Secretariat's estimates assume that the market

Secretariat estimates of car density car park and total demand
EEC, TEN - 1985-2000

Year End December	Car density	Popln.	Car park	Demand		
				New	Replacement	Total
	Cars '000 people	million	'000	'000	'000	'000
ITALY						
1979 actual	305.5	56.96	17 400	414	979	1 393
1980 actual	315.1	57.10[1]	17 990	590	940	1 530
1985	355.4	58.13	20 659	526	1 006	1 531
1990	389.0	59.15	23 010	417	1 243	1 660
1995	414.8	60.15	24 950	382	1 474	1 856
2000	433.6	61.12	26 502	296	1 572	1 868

Assumptions : Saturation : 500 ; Scrapping Rate : to rise from 1970s average of 4.0 % to 6.0 % by 1995 (i.e. 5.0 % in 1985, 5.5 % in 1990, 6.0 % in 1995) and then remain constant.

DENMARK						
1979 actual	278.0	5.12	1 423	16	111	127
1980 actual	271.2	5.13	1 390	–	74	74
1985	318.1	5.14	1 635	25	112	137
1990	337.6	5.18	1 748	21	120	141
1995	352.0	5.23	1 842	17	127	144
2000	362.9	5.30	1 923	16	133	149

Assumptions : Saturation : 400 ; Scrapping Rate ; to remain at 1974-80 average of 7.0 %.

NETHERLANDS						
1979 actual	298.3	14.08	4 200	184	385	569
1980 actual	307.4	14.15	4 350	150	300	450
1985	349.2	14.48	5 056	132	419	551
1990	382.5	14.77	5 650	112	471	583
1995	408.0	15.15	6 181	102	516	618
2000	427.8	15.53	6 644	92	557	649

Assumptions : Saturation : 500 ; Scrapping Rate : to rise from 1970s average of 8.1 % to 8.5 % by 1985 and thereafter remain constant.

IRELAND						
1979 actual	200.9	3.40	683	43	51	94
1980 actual						94
1985	216.2	3.50	757	29	59	88
1990	239.9	3.68	883	26	69	95
1995	261.1	3.85	1 005	23	79	102
2000	279.1	4.03	1 125	22	88	110

Assumptions : Saturation : 450 ; Scrapping Rate : to rise from 1970s average of 7.5 % to 8.0 % by 1985, and then remain constant.

1. Estimate.

15. At *Roundtable 55* "Forecasting Ownership and Use of Vehicles" ECMT, (Paris 1981).

will adjust over the long term to a saturation level of 400. That is, it is suggested that Denmark's vehicle density will gradually increase in a similar fashion to other countries with high personal incomes, population densities, etc. (e.g. Belgium, the Netherlands). This would also depend, presumably, on some reduction in motoring costs in Denmark over the longer term.

On the above basis, Denmark's vehicle density is projected to rise from around 271 at present to 363 by the year 2000. By this time, it is anticipated that replacement demand will account for almost 90 per cent of demand. The annual scrapping rate is estimated to stabilize at the 1974-80 average (7.0 per cent), i.e. around 1 percentage point lower than the majority of other Western European markets.

In *the Netherlands,* recent growth in vehicle density has been quite substantial, and consistent with a saturation level of 500. Such a level seems a little high given its population density. However the demand estimates have been calculated on this basis – indeed it may well be that the growth path will be accurate to the year 2000 (vehicle density of 428), but after this date, the curve could flatten towards a lower saturation level[16].

By 1985, automobile sales are estimated at around 550 000 units, which implies market growth of about 1 per cent over and above 1975-80 average sales. After 1985, market growth is projected at 1.1 per cent per year, resulting in annual sales of 649 000 by the year 2000. Replacement demand by this time are expected to account for 86 per cent of total sales.

With regard to the Netherlands' scrapping rate, the 1970s average of 8.1 per cent is indicative of a market already past the mid-point of its growth path, and moving towards saturation. The rate is tentatively assumed to rise to 8.5 per cent by 1985, and then level off, consistent with an average vehicle lifetime of about 11.8 years.

In *Ireland,* sales are projected at around 90 000 units by 1985, which is slightly below the 1979-80 level. This estimate may be a little on the pessimistic side, given that the projected 1985 vehicle density of 216 seems likely to be reached by 1982. The Secretariat nevertheless feels that a raising of the saturation level (to accommodate the above) would be inconsistent with the United Kingdom experience. In addition the road network in Ireland would probably require substantial upgrading through to the year 2000 to support a vehicle population higher than that forecast.

Beyond 1985, the market is expected to grow at around 1.3 per cent per year, leading to a vehicle population of 1.13 million vehicles by the year 2000. Replacement demand, by this time, is expected to account for 80 per cent of total sales.

The Irish projections are based on the premise that scrapping rates around 1985 will be slightly above those for the 1970s (8.0 per cent compared with 7.5 per cent). It is assumed that the scrapping rate will remain at around 8.0 per cent beyond 1985 which is in line with the U.K. scenario and Secretariat calculations of possible average vehicle lifetimes by this time.

In *Belgium,* the automobile market is projected to grow at about 1.3 per cent per year after 1985. By the year 2000, sales are expected to total 510 000, which is some 80 000 units higher than the cyclical peaks of 1977-79. A slight fall in scrapping rates (see below) and slow population growth would seem to be the major contributing factors in this regard.

Secretariat estimates of Belgium's scrapping rates indicate that they are the highest in the world (average of 10.2 per cent per year in the 1970s). The reasons would probably lie mainly with the high traffic density and associated wear and tear on vehicles and the relative cheapness of cars; the stringent annual inspection procedures for cars more than four years old might also be relevant. A scrapping rate of around 10.0 per cent is projected over the long-term.

In *Luxembourg,* growth in vehicle density has been quite spectacular in the last few years; between 1977 and 1979, the number of vehicles per thousand population increased from 391 to 449. The 1979 level was already equivalent to the Secretariat 1985 estimate based on a saturation of 550. Accordingly, a saturation level of 600 was adopted, together with a high scrapping profile, similar to that of Belgium.

The situation after 1990 shows minimal sales to new customers (as saturation is approached) with a consequent levelling out of annual sales to about 20 000 vehicles. This is a little less than the high sales levels of 1979-80. It should be borne in mind however that the possibe transhipment to other European countries of cars sold in Luxembourg is not taken into account here.

Greece is presently at about the same stage of motorism as Portugal and Yugoslavia. Scrapping rates have been tentatively set at around the Portuguese level; this was necessary since available data indicates a zero scrapping rate. Imports of second-hand vehicles (e.g. by expatriate Greek workers returning from Western Europe) may possibly account for this, by adding to vehicle stock growth and thus disguising the real level of scrapping.

During the 1985-2000 period, automobile demand in Greece is projected to grow at 3.4 per cent annually, leading to an approximately doubling of present sales by the year 2000. Replacement demand by this stage should represent some 60 per cent of total demand.

---

16. That is, as a result of the stabilization of the age structure of the car park.

Secretariat estimates of car density
car park and total demand
EEC Countries - 1985-2000

Year End December	Car density	Popln.	Car park	Demand		
				New	Replacement	total
	Cars '000 people	million	'000	'000	'000	'000
BELGIUM						
1979 actual	312.2	9.85	3 077	104	320	424
1980 actual	319.1	9.90[1]	3 159	82	317	399
1985	345.6	10.10	3 491	84	341	425
1990	376.2	10.31	3 879	78	380	458
1995	401.0	10.54	4 227	69	416	485
2000	421.2	10.79	4 545	62	448	510

Assumptions : Saturation : 520 ; Scrapping Rate : to fall from 1970s average of 10.2 % to 10.0 % by 1985.

Year End December	Car density	Popln.	Car park	New	Replacement	total
LUXEMBOURG						
1979 actual	449.3	0.37	164	11	12	23
1980 actual						22
1985						19[1]
1990	478.5	0.36	173	2	17	19
1995	503.3	0.37	184	2	18	20
2000	522.6	0.37	193	1	19	20

Assumptions : Saturation : 600 ; Scrapping Rate : to rise from 1970s average of 8.0 % to 10.0 % by 1990 (i.e. 1985 = 9.0 %).

Year End December	Car density	Popln.	Car park	New	Replacement	total
GREECE						
1979 actual	88.8	9.45	839	94	2	96
1980 actual	92.6	9.50	880			n.a.
1985	115.2	9.67	1 114	70	42	112
1990	148.1	9.98	1 478	73	61	134
1995	179.8	10.29	1 850	73	83	160
2000	209.0	10.61	2 217	73	107	180

Assumptions : Saturation : 430 ; Scrapping Rate : to rise from 4.0 % in 1985 to 5.0 % in the year 2000 (i.e. 1990 = 4.33 %, 1995 = 4.66 %).

1. Estimate.

Scandinavia

Sweden is presently exhibiting the characteristics of a mature automobile market. While the market grew strongly during the 1960s and early 1970s, car ownership has levelled off in recent years to around 350 vehicles per thousand population.

On the other hand, the level of car ownership in *Norway* and *Finland* has continued to increase steadily in recent years. This trend, which has been in spite of a general slowdown in new registrations, has largely been the result of a recent decline (presumably short-term) in scrapping rates. Secretariat estimates suggest that the number of vehicles scrapped in Norway and Finland during 1978-1979 were some 43 per cent and 23 per cent below the respective levels of 1976-77.

The Scandinavian countries have, in fact, the lowest rates of vehicle scrapping among the developed markets. In the 1970s the annual proportion of vehicles scrapped were as follows: Finland (5.0 per cent), Norway (5.4 per cent) and Sweden (6.6 per cent). One possible reason for Scandinavia's low scrapping rates may be the market penetration of Volvo and Saab who ranked first and fifth in a recent survey of average vehicle lifetimes[17].

While the scrapping rates for Finland and Norway are below Sweden's, it has probably little to do with any particular climatic, economic or other factors. The explanation would lie mainly with the fact that Finland and Norway are lower down the saturation curve, and hence their car parks are not as mature (and liable to scrapping) as those of Sweden. In this regard, it is assumed that as the Finnish and Norwegian markets approach saturation, their scrapping rates will align to the Swedish rate.

17. See the Table 2 of this Annex.

Secretariat estimates of car density
car park and total demand
Scandinavia - 1985-2000

Year End December	Car density	Popln.	Car park	Demand		
				New	Replacement	Total
	Cars '000 people	million	'000	'000	'000	'000

SWEDEN

1979 actual	345.5	8.30	2 868	12	203	215
1980 actual	346.5	8.32	2 883	15	178	193
1985	387.5	8.35	3 234	45	210	255
1990	407.3	8.43	3 434	38	224	262
1995	422.5	8.56	3 615	35	236	271
2000	434.2	8.72	3 784	33	248	281

Assumptions : Saturation : 480 ; Scrapping Rate : constant at 6.6 %.

NORWAY

1979 actual	291.6	4.08	1 190	43	46	89
1980 actual	301.3	4.10	1 234	44	52	96
1985 *	299.2	4.14	1 239	28	74	102
1990	325.0	4.22	1 372	25	88	113
1995	346.0	4.31	1 492	23	97	120
2000	363.0	4.43	1 606	22	104	126

Assumptions : Saturation : 450 ; Scrapping Rate : historical level of 5.4 % (1970s) assumed to align with Swedish rate of 6.6 % by 1990 ; hence 6.0 % (1985) and 6.6 % (1990-2000).

FINLAND

1979 actual	245.1	4.77	1 170	54	46	100
1980 actual	256.2	4.79	1 226	56	47	103
1985	273.6	4.92	1 345	36	76	112
1990	302.6	4.99	1 509	30	98	128
1995	326.4	5.05	1 649	26	107	133
2000	345.8	5.12	1 769	22	115	137

Assumptions : Saturation : 440 ; Scrapping Rate : historical level of 5.0 % (1970s) assumed to align with Swedish rate by 1990 ; hence 5.8 % (1985) and 6.6 % (1990-2000).

* In view of 1980 actual performance, the 1985 projection (based on long-term trends) could be an under-estimation.

In summary, aggregate demand in the Scandinavian region is projected to grow from 393 000 units in 1980 to around 544 000 in the year 2000 (an annual growth of about 1.7 per cent over the period). By the year 2000, replacement purchases are expected to account for 90 per cent of total automobile sales.

Rest of Europe

In *Austria,* the present vehicle density is a little above the predicted trend, with the result that the 1985 sales estimate of 232 000 units may be a little on the conservative side. Beyond 1985, the market is projected to grow at around 1.8 per cent per year. By the year 2000, it is expected that annual sales will approach 300 000 units, of which 254 000 (or 85 per cent) will be replacement sales.

With regard to underlying assumptions, the estimated saturation level of 520 (compared with 300 at present) takes account of Austria's relatively high GDP per capita, and lower level of urbanisation than many other European countries (e.g. Benelux, the Federal Republic of Germany, United Kingdom). The scrapping rate is assumed to align with the West German rate by 1990.

The *Swiss* vehicle stock has grown substantially since the early 1960s, with the result that vehicle ownership per thousand people has doubled since 1966 (339 in 1979). Thus, over the last few years, vehicle ownership levels have moved above the trend (see country graph) which means that the 1985 sales estimates should be treated with caution.

Beyond 1990, the market is projected to grow at around 1.0 per cent, culminating in annual sales of 294 000 units by the year 2000. Replacement demand will represent 87 per cent of total demand by this stage.

Scrapping rates in Switzerland are already high (8.8 per cent in the 1970s) compared with most other European countries – high incomes and a concomitantly weak used vehicle market might be the main

Secretariat estimates of car density
car park and total demand
Other Europe - 1985-2000

Year End December	Car density	Popln.	Car park	Demand		
				New	Replacement	Total
	Cars '000 people	million	'000	'000	'000	'000
AUSTRIA						
1979 actual	285.2	7.50	2 139	99	115	214
1980 actual	299.7	7.51	2 247	109	119	228
1985	326.2	7.52	2 453	63	169	232
1990	362.2	7.54	2 731	54	214	268
1995	391.4	7.64	2 988	49	235	284
2000	414.8	7.77	3 222	45	254	299

Assumptions : Saturation : 520 ; Scrapping Rate : to rise from 1970s average of 6.1 % to German rate of 8.0 % by 1990 (i.e. 1985 = 7.1 %).

SWITZERLAND						
1979 actual	338.9	6.36	2 154	100	180	280
1980 actual	353.3	6.36	2 247	93	188	281
1985	358.9	6.31	2 265	60[1]	195	255[1]
1990	393.1	6.38	2 508	47	217	264
1995	422.0	6.47	2 732	44	237	281
2000	446.5	6.58	2 936	39	255	294

Assumptions : Saturation : 600 ; Scrapping Rate : constant at 1970s average of 8.8 %.

SPAIN						
1979 actual	189.7	37.20	7 058	527	48	575
1980 actual	201.3	37.55[1]	7 557	500	4	504
1985	256.8	39.10	10 041	526	219	745
1990	304.7	40.69	12 398	305	447	752
1995	329.5	42.15	13 888	283	738	1 019
2000	349.7	43.49	15 208	250	972	1 222

Assumptions : Saturation : to follow a 530 growth path until vehicle density of 300 is reached (1989) thereafter to follow a 450 growth path ; Scrapping Rate : to rise from 1970s average of 0.9 % to 6.5 % by the year 2000 (i.e. 1985 = 2.3 %, 1990 = 3.7 %, 1995 = 5.1 %).

1. Estimate.

explanations in this regard. Future rates are assumed to remain at around 8.8 per cent (vehicle life equivalent of 11.4 years) which is slightly higher than those for the Federal Republic of Germany and Austria.

In *Spain,* the rapid growth in the number of passenger vehicles per person since the early sixties is consistent with an eventual saturation of 530. However the Secretariat believes this is a little optimistic, and the assumption has been made that once an ownership level of 300 is reach (by 1989), the approach path will adjust to a saturation of 450.

With regard to scrapping rates, these have been very low (0.9 per cent per year during the 1970s), the result of Spain's late but strong growth in motorism. It is hypothesised that the Spanish rates will align with those of Italy by the year 2000.

On the above basis, the Spanish market is projected to grow by around 4.6 per cent between 1980 and 2000. By this time, the car park will be approximately double the present size, and replacement demand will represent some 81 per cent of total demand.

In *Portugal,* automobile sales by 1985 are projected at around 100 000 units, which is some 45 000 units above the 1978-80 average. The market will remain in a growth phase over the next two decades; annual growth in demand is estimated at approximately 3.2 per cent between 1985 and the year 2000. By this time, replacement demand will still only account for 63 per cent of total demand.

The 3.5 per cent scrapping rate for Portugal (as calculated) is assumed to rise during the 1980s and 1990s to around 5.0 per cent by the year 2000. It is not expected to reach the rates of more developed markets in the region because of the continuing growth of car ownership (see France footnote).

The scant data available for *Turkey* necessitates the arbitrary judgement that annual scrapping rate is presently around 3.5 per cent and that it will follow the Portuguese trend in the 1980s and 1990s.

Secretariat estimates of car density
car park and total demand
Other Europe - 1985-2000

Year End December	Car density	Popln.	Car park	Demand		
				New	Replacement	Total
	Cars '000 people	million	'000	'000	'000	'000
PORTUGAL						
1979 actual	92.0	9.92	912	24	28	52
1980 actual						
1985	118.2	10.40	1 230	55	46	101
1990	139.2	10.89	1 516	57	62	119
1995	158.8	11.37	1 805	58	81	139
2000	177.0	11.83	2 095	59	102	161

Assumptions : Saturation : 350 ; Scrapping Rate : to rise from 3.5 % (1970s average) to 5.0 % by year 2000 (i.e. 1985 = 3.88 %. 1990 = 4.25 %, 1995 = 4.63 %).

TURKEY						
1979 actual	15.1	43.58	659			55
1980 actual	16.0	44.44	711			33
1985	18.7	51.84	969	83	34	117
1990	25.0	58.13	1 453	105	57	162
1995	32.2	64.29	2 070	133	90	223
2000	39.9	69.96	2 791	146	132	278

Assumptions : Saturation : 400 ; Scrapping Rate : as for Portugal.

ICELAND						
1979 actual	352.4	0.23	80			n.a.
1980 actual						n.a.
1985	366.8	0.24	89	2	6	8
1990	399.5	0.26	102	2	7	9
1995	426.0	0.27	114	2	7	9
2000	447.5	0.28	124	2	9	11

Assumptions : Saturation : 550 ; Scrapping Rate ; as for Sweden, 6.6 % constant.

YUGOSLAVIA						
1979 actual	102.7	22.26	2 285			n.a.
1980 actual	107.8	22.43	2 417			n.a.
1985	151.4	23.35	3 535	210	129	339
1990	187.9	24.20	4 547	198	185	383
1995	218.9	24.97	5 466	177	245	422
2000	244.4	25.72	6 286	159	306	465

Assumptions : Saturation : 350 ; Scrapping Rate : as for Portugal.

Market growth in Turkey is thus projected at approximately 6.0 per cent between 1985-2000, leading to replacement sales equal to 47 per cent of total sales by the end of the century.

In *Iceland*, sales are expected to be around 11 000 by the year 2000. This is based on the assumption that Iceland will have a fairly high saturation level (550), as a result of its reasonably high GDP per capita and the lesser importance of public transport in Iceland.

In *Yugoslavia*, sales are projected to grow by around 2.1 per cent annually between 1985 and 2000. Since the Secretariat has been unable to gather historical sales data, the above estimate is based on likely scrapping rates for Portugal, which is at a similar stage of development to that of Yugoslavia.

By the year 2000, Yugoslavia is projected to have a substantially higher vehicle density than Portugal however (244 compared with 177). The main explanation in this regard is Yugoslavia's steeper sales growth curve since the early 1960s. Replacement demand is predicted to account for around 57 per cent of sales by the end of the century.

OECD Pacific

In *Japan*, the growth of motorism has been very rapid since the mid-sixties – rising from 28 cars per thousand people in 1966 to 202 in 1980. As a result of this growth, the lowest saturation level which could be fitted to the data was 610. The Secretariat believes that such a saturation level is unrealistic, given the level of urbanisation in Japan. It is assumed that Japanese car ownership will follow a growth path equivalent to a saturation of 610 until 1986, when a level of 300 is expected to be reached. In support of this assumption is the prospect of continuing growth in Japan's GDP capita, and the Japanese authorities' opinion that substantial scope for further growth of motorism exists in the rural areas of Japan. Beyond 1986, it is assumed that the growth path will follow a saturation level of 450, similar to the United Kingdom.

Scrapping rates in Japan over the last decade have been relatively high (7.1 per cent) considering that the automobile market has been growing strongly from a low vehicle density base. Data concerning vehicle lifetimes indicate a present age of 8.4 years, rising to 9.4 years by 1985 and 10.6 years by 1990. This suggests that scrapping rates will be around 9.0 per cent by 1990[18].

On the basis of the above, automobile demand in Japan is likely to be quite strong until the mid-1980s (perhaps running at 7 per cent to 8 per cent annually) due to continuing high levels of new demand, as well as strengthening replacement demand. By the late 1980s, the growth phase of new demand is expected to be nearing its end, but a 68 per cent larger vehicle stock by 1990 should ensure replacement demand of around 3.5 million units annually. From 1990 onwards, annual market growth is projected to fall back to a typical mature market rate of around 1.2 per cent. By the year 2000 replacement demand is projected at 87 per cent of total demand.

Secretariat estimates of car density car park and total demand

OECD Pacific - 1985-2000

Year End December	Car density	Popln.	Car park	Demand		
				New	Replacement	Total
	Cars '000 people	million	'000	'000	'000	'000
JAPAN						
1979 actual	194.9	116.33	22 667	1 387	1 650	3 037
1980 actual	201.8	117.24[1]	23 660	993	1 861	2 854
1985	287.6	120.04	34 524	1 791	2 619	4 410
1990	322.6	123.07	39 702	757	3 505	4 262
1995	343.1	126.16	43 285	689	3 834	4 523
2000	359.9	129.90	46 499	611	4 130	4 741

Assumptions : Saturation : to follow on 618 growth path until vehicle density of 300 is reached (1986), thereafter to follow a 450 growth path. Scrapping Rate : to rise from 1970s average of 7.1 % to 8.0 % (1985) and 9.0 % (1990) and then remain constant.

AUSTRALIA						
1979 actual	388.7	14.74	5 728	118	343	461
1980 actual	396.3	14.91	5 910	182	271	453
1985	425.8	15.51	6 602	153	368	521
1990	448.0	16.40	7 346	149	443	592
1995	466.0	17.26	8 043	139	522	661
2000	480.0	18.07	8 674	128	564	692

Assumptions : Saturation : 550 ; Scrapping Rate : to rise from 1970s average of 5.3 % to long-term rate of 6.6 % by year 1995 ; hence 5.7 % (1985), 6.15 % (1990) and 6.6 % (1995-2000).

NEW ZEALAND						
1979 actual	398.8	3.13	1 247	11	57	68
1980 actual	n.a.	n.a.	n.a.	n.a.	n.a.	n.a.
1985	432.4	3.48	1 504	36	81	117
1990	455.6	3.64	1 673	34	91	125
1995	473.2	3.86	1 828	30	107	137
2000	486.0	4.04	1 965	25	115	140

Assumptions : Saturation : 550 ; Scrapping Rate ; to rise from 1970s average of 3.4 % to 5.5. % by 1985, and thereafter to be 90 % of Australian rates (i.e. 5.54 % in 1990, 5.94 % from 1995-2000).

1. Estimate.

18. This is less than the reciprocal of 10.6 years (9.43 per cent) in view of the fact that the vehicle stock will be slightly "newer" (and hence scrapping rates slightly lower) than would be the case during a less dynamic market growth phase.

In *Australia,* annual growth in sales has been relatively low (1.2 per cent average) since 1972. However, three factors favour marginally higher demand in the longer term

   i) a projected rise in vehicle scrapping rates from 5.3 per cent during the 1970s to 6.6 per cent by the mid-1990s;
   ii) a likely rate of population growth of 0.9 per cent annually between 1980-2000;
   iii) general rises in real disposable income.

The above influences may foster an underlying growth rate in automobile demand of between 1 per cent and 2 per cent between 1980-2000. By the year 2000, replacement demand is estimated to constitute 85 per cent of total demand, compared with around 65 per cent at present. Vehicle densities are estimated to rise approximately 24 per cent over the same period.

In *New Zealand,* car ownership, as in Australia, is already reasonably high. The dependence of the New Zealand population on the automobile probably stems from the lack of public transport, whereas the Australian situation would be more related to the geographic factor. It is assumed that the New Zealand vehicle density will continue to increase towards a saturation level of 550; the present signs of a relaxation of its import policy towards automobiles would support this eventuality.

Between 1985 and 1995, the New Zealand market is projected to grow by 1.6 per cent annually, tapering off thereafter as saturation is approached. Replacement demand in the year 2000 is estimated at 82 per cent of total demand.

COMECON

Little reliable data exists from which estimates of scrapping rates can be derived for the Comecon countries. The following rates have nevertheless been estimated:

Czechoslovakia: 2.3 per cent per year between 1973-78, and 3.0 per cent in 1979.
Romania: 4 per cent in 1980.
Poland: 3.0 per cent per year between 1976-79,

On this basis, it is estimated that scrapping rates for the USSR and the other Comecon markets is currently around 3.0 per cent and that it will rise to around 5.0 per cent by the year 2000 (same as for Yugoslavia). A low scrapping rate of this order seems reasonable given the fact that car ownership in the Comecon countries will still be low in the year 2000 by Western European standards; since cars are very much status symbols in the Communist bloc this will also ensure that they are kept on the road for as long as possible.

On the above basis, it is estimated that the *USSR* automobile market will grow by 4.8 per cent annually during the period 1985-2000. This is conditional, of course, on demand being matched by supply – which

Secretariat estimates of car density
car park and total demand
Comecon - 1985-2000

Year End December	Car density	Popln.	Car park	Demand		
				New	Replacement	Total
	Cars '000 people	million	'000	'000	'000	'000
USSR						
1979 actual	31.1	268.00	8 254			n.a.
1980 actual						n.a.
1985	38.4	280.62	10 783	793	350	1 143
1990	51.5	292.74	15 076	900	567	1 467
1995	65.4	302.96	19 904	1 001	851	1 852
2000	80.4	312.82	25 151	1 094	1 203	2 297

Assumptions :   Saturation : 350 ; Scrapping Rate : as for « Other Comecon ».

OTHER COMECON (Bulgaria, Czechoslovakia, Poland, East Germany, Romania, Hungary).						
1979 actual	72.9	109.65	7 991			n.a.
1980 actual						n.a.
1985	98.6	113.85	11 226	630	371	1 001
1990	123.0	116.75	14 360	625	549	1 174
1995	146.4	119.40	17 480	611	760	1 371
2000	168.0	122.13	20 518	594	996	1 590

Assumptions :   Saturation : 350 ; Scrapping Rate : to rise from 3.0 % to 5.0 % by the year 2000 (i.e. 1985 = 3.5 %, 1990 = 4.0 %, 1995 = 4.5 %).

essentially depends on planning allocations. This difficulty aside, replacement demand is forecast to account for 52 per cent of total sales by the year 2000.

In the *remaining Comecon countries,* the market is projected to grow by around 3.2 per cent during 1985-2000. By the year 2000, replacement demand is expected to be equivalent to 63 per cent of total demand.

To test the viability of the above demand estimates, the Secretariat has compared its 1985 Total Comecon demand figure with some production forecasts provided by CEDUCEE[19]. Likely 1985 production volumes are as follows: Poland (400 000 units), East Germany (171 000), Romania (62 400), Czechoslovakia (153 800). No forecasts were made for the USSR but on the basis of 1980 production of 1.327 million units a level of, say, 1.5 million can be set for 1985[20]. Totalling these estimates gives a production figure of 2.287 million units. It should be noted that, given the Secretariat 1985 demand estimates for Total Comecon of 2.144 million units, the total surplus available for export would be 143 000 units. In 1978, Comecon exports to the OECD (including Yugoslavia) were of the order of 180 000 units – suggesting perhaps the Secretariat's demand projections may be overly-optimistic, as would be the even higher demand estimates provided in the Interfutures study.

Africa

In the *Republic of South Africa,* market growth through to 1985 is projected to be around 6.0 per cent per annum (the same as in the 1970s), tapering off thereafter to a long-term rate of 3.0 per cent by around 1995. This relatively strong growth will be due to population growth as well as to a 50 per cent rise in vehicle density levels by the year 2000.

The saturation level of 350 assumes that vehicle ownership by the non-white population (currently around 80 per cent of the total) will progressively increase, mainly through purchases in the used-car market. The scrapping rate is projected to increase marginally from an average of 6.2 per cent at present to a level mid-way between most developed countries' rates (i.e. 7.0 per cent).

In the *Rest of Africa,* the market is projected to grow at slightly under 5 per cent per year between 1985-2000, mainly due to strong population growth. The vehicle density will remain low (12.5 vehicles per thousand people in the year 2000).

Secretariat estimates of car density car park and total demand
Africa - 1985-2000

Year End December	Car density	Popln.	Car park	Demand		
				New	Replacement	Total
	Cars '000 people	million	'000	'000	'000	'000
REPUBLIC OF SOUTH AFRICA						
1979 actual	80.7	28.88	2 331	81	131	212
1980 actual	84.0	29.60	2 486	155	122	277
1985	96.8	34.01	3 292	146	220	366
1990	105.8	38.59	4 083	166	274	440
1995	114.4	43.36	4 960	178	335	513
2000	122.6	48.30	5 922	194	401	595

Assumptions : Saturation : 350 ; Scrapping Rate : 1970s average of 6.2 % to rise to 7.0 % by 1985 and then remain constant.

REST OF AFRICA						
1979 actual	8.0	459.6	3 678			n.a.
1980 actual	n.d.					n.a.
1985	8.9	518.7	4 616	236	159	395
1990	10.1	601.0	6 070	291	217	508
1995	11.3	692.2	7 822	347	290	637
2000	12.5	790.2	9 878	403	379	782

Assumptions : Saturation : 100 ; Scrapping Rate : to rise from 3.5 % (1975-80 average) to 4.0 % by year 2000 (i.e. 1985 = 3.63 %, 1990 = 3.75 %, 1995 = 3.88 %).

Note : Population estimates include the Republics of Transkei, Bophuthatswana and Venda.

19. "Les Stratégies Économiques des Pays de l'Est: les Plans 1981-1985", in *Le Courrier des Pays de l'Est* (juillet-août 1981) Centre d'étude et de documentation sur l'USSR, la Chine et l'Europe de l'Est (Paris).
20. Bulgaria and Hungary are not automobile producers – their imports will chiefly come from other COMECON countries.

Scrapping rates in the Rest of Africa have been estimated at around 3.5 per cent per year in the 1975-1980 period. This figure is based on the scrapping rates for three country markets, namely Nigeria (3.8 per cent), Morocco (2.2 per cent) and the Ivory Coast (3.4 per cent) which together account for one quarter of the region's vehicle stock. Since this aggregate market will still be in an infant stage by the year 2000, scrapping rates are likely to increase only slowly over the period, to perhaps around 4.0 per cent.

Latin America

For *Brazil*, it is assumed that the 1976-77 scrapping rates of around 3.0 per cent are applicable for the 1976-80 period[21] and that they will progressively increase to 5.0 per cent by the year 2000 (similar to those of Comecon).

Taking the above into account, the Brazilian market will perform strongly. New (first-time) consumers will play an important role, as a result of the growth phase of the market and population growth. Likely market growth is estimated at between 5 and 6 per cent over the period 1985-2000. These estimates are tentative at this stage, mainly because the projected growth of motorism (29 million vehicles by the year 2000) would need to be sustained by real GDP growth of the order of 5-6 per cent per year.

In *Argentina*, market growth is projected at approximately 3.4 per cent over the 1985-2000 period. This is considerably below the Brazil projection mainly because of Argentina's slower population growth (about half the Brazilian rate) and more moderate approach path.

**Secretariat estimates of car density
car park and total demand
Latin America - 1985-2000**

Year End Decembre	Car density	Popln.	Car park	Demand		
				New	Replacement	Total
	Cars '000 people	million	'000	'000	'000	'000
BRAZIL						
1979 actual	58.2	144.0[1]	8 149	645	34	679
1980 actual	n.a.					n.a.
1985	79.4	147.0	11 672	868	378	1 246
1990	99.4	167.9	16 689	1 082	624	1 706
1995	119.1	190.6	22 700	1 273	964	2 223
2000	137.9	214.9	29 635	1 432	1 410	2 833

Assumptions : Saturation : 350 ; Scrapping Rate : to rise from 3.0 % (1976-80) to 5.0 % by year 2000 (i.e. 1985 = 3.5 %, 1990 = 4.0 %, 1995 = 4.5 %).

Year End Decembre	Car density	Popln.	Car park	Demand		
ARGENTINA						
1979 actual	106.4	26.89	2 860	131	57	188
1980 actual	110.5	27.20[1]	3 005	145	79	224
1985	137.0	28.83	3 950	178	132	310
1990	159.5	30.33	4 838	179	194	373
1995	180.0	31.71	5 708	171	267	438
2000	198.4	32.92	6 531	152	351	503

Assumptions : Saturation : 350 ; Scrapping Rate : to rise from 3.0 % to 5.5 % by the year 2000 (i.e. 1985 = 3.5 %, 1990 = 4.16 %, 1995 = 4.83 %).

Year End Decembre	Car density	Popln.	Car park	Demand		
REST OF SOUTH AMERICA						
1979 actual	30.2	90.50	2 732			n.a.
1980 actual	n.a.					
1985	33.0	105.56	3 483	181	66	247
1990	37.7	118.85	4 481	206	103	309
1995	42.3	133.85	5 662	246	152	398
2000	46.8	148.91	6 969	263	215	478

Assumptions : Saturation : 200 ; Scrapping Rate : to rise from 2.0 % in 1985 to 3.2 % by year 2000 (i.e. 1990 = 2.4 %, 1995 = 2.8 %).

1. Estimate.

21. Sales data beyond 1977 are not presently available to the Secretariat. The available data for the 1970-75 period suggests that scrapping rates in Brazil were minimal.

The above estimates are based on scrapping rates rising from a present rate of slightly under 3.0 per cent to 5.5 per cent by the year 2000. This latter figure is higher than that assumed for Brazil, Comecon, etc. because of the likelihood that the Argentinian market will be approaching the mature phase by the year 2000.

The *Rest of South America* market mainly comprises Venezuela, Chile, Colombia, Peru and Uruguay. Vehicle densities, in aggregate, are likely to remain relatively low in the period under review. By the year 2000, the vehicle density will be approaching 50 per thousand people, giving rise to annual demand of almost 500 000 units. This represents an annual growth in sales of 4.7 per cent between 1985-2000; by this time replacement demand will still only account for 45 per cent of total demand.

Since little reliable data exists for the calculation of scrapping rates, the same schedule as that for Other Central America was used; that is, rising from 2.0 per cent to 3.2 per cent by the year 2000.

The historical data for *Mexico*, although not strictly accurate, suggest that the scrapping rate in the late 1970s was between 1 and 2 per cent. It is assumed that it will have reached 2.5 per cent by 1985 and rise thereafter to 5.0 per cent by the year 2000 (similar to Brazil). The very high population growth as forecast for Mexico does cast some doubt on the saturation level used (350), particularly since the infrastructural development required to support 12 million vehicles by the year 2000 will be substantial.

However, over the medium term (1985) a sales projection of 450 000 units (implying an annual market growth of 10 per cent) could be easily reached given a recent prognosis of the EIU:

"increased consumer confidence in a booming economy fueled by new oil discoveries and backed by big investments in the motor industry, pushed sales in 1979 above their 1974 peak level. All industries sectors... and the corresponding government departments are unanimously and confidently forecasting medium-term growth rates of around 15-17 per cent[22]."

Beyond 1985, the Secretariat estimates likely market growth at around 7.0 per cent; and by the year 2000 replacement sales should almost be equal to new market demand.

In *Rest of Central America*, a continuing low level of motorism is expected, with the majority of automobile demand coming from first-time purchasers. Annual sales growth is nevertheless projected at 4.5 per cent, culminating in aggregate demand of 371 000 units by the year 2000.

No data were available within the Secretariat to enable the calculation of scrapping rates for Central America. However, given the low personal incomes in much of this region and its low stage of motorism,

Secretariat estimates of car density car park and total demand
Latin America - 1985-2000

Year End December	Car density	Popln.	Car park	Demand		
				New	Replacement	Total
	Cars '000 people	million	'000	'000	'000	'000
MEXICO						
1979 actual	50.0	68.84	3 080	200[1]	67[1]	267
1980 actual	n.a.					n.a.
1985	57.2	84.25	4 819	338	112	450
1990	68.3	99.21	6 776	425	211	636
1995	79.6	115.86	9 224	537	361	898
2000	90.7	134.19	12 171	629	577	1 206

Assumptions : Saturation : 350 ; Scrapping Rate : to rise to 2.5 % in 1985 and continue to 5.0 % by the year 2000 (i.e. 1990 = 3.33 %, 1995 = 4.16 %).

REST OF CENTRAL AMERICA (including the Caribbean)						
1979 actual	37.5	52.81	1 982			n.a.
1980 actual	n.a.					n.a.
1985	44.8	60.55	2 713	132	59	191
1990	51.0	67.73	3 454	162	86	248
1995	56.9	75.59	4 301	174	120	294
2000	62.8	84.09	5 281	209	162	371

Assumptions : Saturation : 200 ; Scrapping Rate : to rise from 2.0 % (actual tax) to 3.2 % by the year 2000 (i.e. 1985 = 2.3 %, 1990 = 2.6 %, 1995 = 2.4 %).

1. Estimate.

22. *Motor Business,* 1980. Economist Intelligence Unit.

present rates are probably no more than 2.0 per cent. It was assumed that scrapping rates would gradually increase to 3.2 per cent by the year 2000. This latter rate is roughly that found in less developed countries whose vehicle densities are around 60-70 per thousand people.

Asia

The *Indian* market is still very much in the infant stage and is likely to remain so during the remainder of this century. Indeed, sales and vehicle densities since around 1973-74 have shown little or no growth.

However, in terms of the future, India's Fifth Five Year Plan (1974-79) did provide almost $3 billion for expenditure on the road network, the major part of which was earmarked for the surfacing of 100 000 kilometres of roads. Infrastructural development of this sort indicates a distinct shift in the Government's attitude towards the automobile, given that India has traditionally relied on the railway system as the major mode of passenger and goods movement.

The Secretariat's demand estimates rest very much on the Indian Government's continuation of its new policy orientation. The projections indicate a likely growth in automobile demand of about 3.5 per cent per year between 1985-2000. Since the vehicle density is only expected to increase slowly (from 15 to 21 cars per thousand people) this market growth will emanate from increases in the car-driving population and, to a lesser extent, from increases in replacement demand.

Annual scrapping rates in India were approximately 2.1 per cent during the late 1970s (2.2 per cent for the whole of the 1970s). It is hypothesised that the 1985 level will still be around this level, rising to 3.0 per cent by the year 2000. The latter rate is similar to that adopted for the less developed regions of South America (3.2 per cent). The low-variant population projection of the U.N. was used to allow for recent signs of a slowdown in India's population growth.

Secretariat estimates of car density
car park and total demand
Asia - 1985-2000

Year End December	Car density Cars '000 people	Popln. million	Car park '000	Demand		
				New '000	Replacement '000	Total '000
INDIA						
1979 actual	12.0	678.2	820	29	–	29
1980 actual	12.0	690.4	830[1]	29	1	30
1985	15.7	772.6	1 213	54	24	78
1990	17.5	847.7	1 483	59	34	93
1995	19.3	921.3	1 778	64	46	110
2000	21.1	990.5	2 090	68	61	129

Assumptions : Saturation : 100 ; Scrapping Rate : to rise from 2.1 % in 1985 to 3.0 % in the year 2000 (i.e. 1990 = 2.4 %, 1995 = 2.7 %).

Year End December	Car density Cars '000 people	Popln. million	Car park '000	Demand		
				New '000	Replacement '000	Total '000
ASEAN (Malaysia, Singapore, Thailand, Indonesia and the Philippines)						
1979 actual	8.2	260.0	2 124			230[1]
1980 actual	n.a.					n.a.
1985	10.8	304.9	3 793	196	99	295
1990	13.0	340.4	4 425	259	145	404
1995	15.3	375.2	5 741	289	203	492
2000	17.7	407.5	7 213	311	276	587

Assumptions : Saturation : 200 ; Scrapping Rate : to rise from 3.2 % in 1985 to 4.0 % in the year 2000 (i.e. 1990 = 3.47 %, 1995 = 3.73 %).

Year End December	Car density Cars '000 people	Popln. million	Car park '000	Demand		
				New '000	Replacement '000	Total '000
REST OF SOUTH EAST ASIA (mainly South Korea, Taiwan, Hong Kong, Vietnam)						
1979 actual	5.7	158.3	900			n.a.
1980 actual	n.a.					n.a.
1985	6.9	179.6	1 239	77	60	137
1990	8.4	198.8	1 670	91	85	176
1995	10.1	219.0	2 212	132	119	251
2000	11.9	238.0	2 832	143	162	305

Assumptions : Saturation : 200 ; Scrapping Rate : to rise from 5.0 % in 1985 to 6.0 % in the year 2000 (i.e. 1990 = 5.33 %, 1995 = 5.6 %).

1. Estimate.

47

The expansion of the ASEAN market has slowed considerably in recent years, partly as a result of high vehicle prices and related taxes. Supply shortages have also been a limiting factor due to relatively restrictive import policies in much of the area.

Singapore's approach is not wholly typical of the region, but is worth noting since high taxes on the ownership and use of cars did actually check the growth of vehicle numbers between 1974 and 1977. Registration fees were reported as having been increased an additional 54 per cent in 1979, and a scheme now operates to encourage the replacement of older cars (fees rise as the vehicle ages). The measures have led to a fall to 4.3 years in the average age of the car park[23]; however the intended reduction in vehicle numbers has not occurred.

Taking the above developments into account suggests that present scrapping rates in Singapore are around Western European levels. However, in the other four ASEAN member countries, scrapping rates remain low. Some rough calculations indicate annual rates of around 4.0 per cent in Malaysia, 3.2 per cent in the Philippines and somewhere between 2 and 3 per cent in Thailand. In terms of the aggregate ASEAN market, it has been assumed that present scrapping rates are about 3.2 per cent and that these will progressively rise to 4.0 per cent by the year 2000[24].

Historical developments of vehicle densities in the ASEAN bloc suggest a doubling to 17.7 vehicles per thousand by the year 2000; for this to be achieved will probably require some major changes in the approach of governments and manufacturers to the market. Nevertheless, on this basis, automobile sales growth is projected at around 5.0 per cent per year between 1985-2000. The 1990 sales estimate of 404 000 is equivalent to the market potential as estimated by foreign manufacturers were import restrictions to be lifted[25].

The *Rest of South East Asia* chiefly comprises the markets of Taiwan (currently accounting for 36 per cent of the region's vehicles), South Korea (27 per cent), Hong Kong (18 per cent) and Vietman (7 per cent). Of these, the markets of Taiwan and South Korea should continue their strong growth in line with likely developments in GDP per capita – substantial growth in the Hong Kong market will be pre-empted by its high population density.

Scattered data suggest that scrapping rates in the Republic of Korea and Taiwan are somewhat higher at present than for most of the ASEAN countries, approximately 4 per cent per annum. This may be due to a narrower car-driving population profile, in particular because of various government motoring taxes[26].

Based on trends in other similar markets, scrapping rates in the Rest of South Asia market are projected to rise slightly to around 5.0 per cent by 1985, and then edge towards 6 per cent over the longer term. The Secretariat projections hence suggest a likely market growth of 5.5 per cent per year for the region between 1985-2000. By this time, the annual passenger car market is expected to be around 300 000 units, or some 225 per cent larger than that at present.

The future direction of the *Middle South Asia* market hinges mainly on Iran (currently accounting for 71 per cent of the region's vehicle stocks), Pakistan (18 per cent) and Sri Lanka (5 per cent). The present situation in Iran obviously introduces uncertainty into any demand projections.

Nevertheless, on the basis of past trends, the annual sales in this region are projected at around 740 000 units by the year 2000. This represents a market growth of 6.5 per cent over the 1985-2000 period.

No data were available from which scrapping rates could be derived for this region – those for the ASEAN market were substituted. It should be noted that the saturation level adopted for this region (100) is lower than that for ASEAN and Rest of South East Asia (200), in spite of the fact that existing vehicle densities are approximately the same. The main reason for this is that Middle South Asia population is largely Islamic, and its religious precepts exclude women from driving an automobile.

The *Middle East* market covers a range of rather non-comparable country situations. The major country markets, based on the size of vehicle fleets, are Saudi Arabia (21 per cent of total region), Kuwait (20 per cent), Israel (19 per cent), Lebanon (17 per cent) and Iraq (10 per cent).

The unequal distribution of wealth in countries such as Saudi Arabia and Kuwait is a major factor likely to block the growth of motorism. Moreover, because of this income gap, the used car market is not strong.

Weather factors also tend to ensure that scrapping rates are relatively high. A recent JETRO paper[27] contended that, in the Middle East, "there is a greater demand for new cars because of weather conditions which make it necessary to replace the old cars after two or three years of use on the average". This accords

---

23. *Far Eastern Economic Review*, 27th February, 1981.
24. Scrapping rates in Indonesia, the second largest market in ASEAN, are probably quite low because of lower personal incomes.
25. *Far Eastern Economic Review*, 27th February, 1982.
26. In this regard, it is instructive to note the situation in South Korea where the Far Eastern Economic Review recently concluded:

"Given the exorbitant cost of buying and maintaing a car, expanding the domestic base could prove diffiicult. Manufacturers and purchasers alike both suffer from 32 differnt kinds of tax levied on producing, purchasing and maintaining a car... One company figured that, at the very least, an income of WON 1 million per month would be required for a household to buy and maintain a vehicle. Presently, South Korea's average yearly per capita is WON 1.3 million.

"Another ownership expense is that of the driver (i.e. chauffeur) – hitherto customary, due to insurance regulations, traffic accident liability and the abiding Confucian belief that driving is a task only for the lower classes." (*Far Eastern Economic Review*, 27th February, 1982).

27. Toshio Miki (Jetro) "Japanese Automakers focussing on Middle East market", in DJIT, No. 155, 1980.

**Secretariat estimates of car density
car park and total demand**

Asia - 1985-2000

Year End December	Car density	Popln.	Car park	Demand		
				New	Replacement	Total
	Cars '000 people	million	'000	'000	'000	'000

MIDDLE SOUTH ASIA (principally Iran, Pakistan, Sri Lanka ; excluding India)

Year End December	Car density	Popln.	Car park	New	Replacement	Total
1979 actual	7.6	258.0	1 965			n.a.
1980 actual	n.a.					n.a.
1985	8.5	318.6	2 708	212	80	292
1990	10.7	375.3	4 016	306	129	435
1995	13.0	437.8	5 619	382	198	580
2000	15.4	504.9		449	293	742

Assumptions :   Saturation : 100 ; Scrapping Rate : same as for ASEAN.

MIDDLE EAST (principally the Arab countries, excluding Egypt, plus Israel).

Year End December	Car density	Popln.	Car park	New	Replacement	Total
1979 actual	36.2	52.06	1 882			435[1]
1980 actual	n.a.					n.a.
1985	40.8	60.75	2 479	190	465	655
1990	52.0	72.70	3 780	250	618	868
1995	61.6	83.90	5 168	296	792	1 088
2000	71.5	95.75	6 846	355	974	1 329

Assumptions :   Saturation : 350 ; Scrapping Rate : to fall from 20 % in 1980 to 15.0 % by the year 2000
(i.e. 1985 = 18.75 %, 1990 = 17.5 %, 1995 = 16.25 %).

1. Estimate.

with a EIU report[28] of vehicle dealers in the United Arab Emirates attributing an average life of two years to every vehicle sold.

The Secretariat, while not doubting the above quotations, believes that the average vehicle lifetimes would be higher in the poorer Middle East countries. Arriving at a scrapping rate for the whole region is obviously difficult. On the basis that Saudi Arabia and the UAE possibly account for 70 per cent of the region's sales, and that the average vehicle lifetime in the remaining countries is somewhere around 8-10 years, the present scrapping rate for the whole Middle East market is assumed to be 20 per cent at present. It is hypothesised that this rate will fall to around 15.0 per cent by the year 2000 as car ownership in the middle-income groups gradually rises; that is, motorists in these groups would be expected to maintain their vehicles for longer than would wealthy motorists.

The saturation level of 350 adopted for the Middle East may be a little high given the Islamic religion's ban on women motorists. However, this influence might be offset if a redistribution of income took place in the future across a broader population base. The saturation level used is, nevertheless, not critically important over a 20 year time period in regions at a relatively low stage of motorism.

Given the above, the Middle East market is projected to grow at around 5.0 per cent between 1985-2000. By this time, annual demand is expected to be around 1.3 million units, or three times the present level.

The remaining country markets are China and North Korea.

There is no private automobile ownership in China – the only passenger cars in use are those owned by government departments, enterprises and diplomatic missions. The stock of such vehicles was approximately 50 000 at end 1979, having grown at around 7 per cent annually during the 1970s. The present passenger vehicle/population rate is about one vehicle per 20 000 persons.

Annual data for passenger vehicle demand are not readily available. Judging by some very approximate figures of passenger vehicle stocks, an annual demand of somewhere around 5 000 vehicles would be an upper limit during the early 1980s. This is in line with production estimates of around 4 000 passenger vehicles for China in 1979[29].

However, there is little likelihood of a takeoff in growth of automobile demand in China prior to the year 2000. While the network of motorable roads increased ten-fold from 80 000 Km in 1949 to 870 000 Km in 1979, in terms of spatial density, China's road system remains one of the least developed in the world. Moreover, the roads are generally of a low standard as regards bridge capacity and design, pavement condition and strength.

28. "Motor Bulletin", 1978, Economist Intelligence Unit.
29. *China Socialist Economic Development,* Annex F. World Bank, June 1981.

Perhaps the major drawback to the development of motorism in China however rests with a certain cultural indifference to the automobile. This probably underpins the Chinese authorities' ban on personal automobile ownership and its commitment to rail travel as the primary means of personal transportation. In brief, the development of motorism, at least on any scale, is some way off in China. Any such development will first require a basic shift in community attitudes and/or political philosophy, not to mention further growth in real disposable incomes.

It is assumed that the Chinese situation also applies to North Korea.

Sensitivity Analysis

Table 3 shows the various demand projections for each country/region for 1985, 1990 and 2000. The "medium" variant represents the demand estimates according to the assumptions outlined in the preceding section.

The "high" and "low" variants indicated in Table 3 related to scrapping rates set at one percentage point above and below those underlying the country projections. The data illustrate that a relatively small change in scrapping rates can significantly change the demand scenario. For example, the "high" scrapping variant for 1990 gives total world demand of 41.8 million units, which is some 4.1 million units above the medium variant.

This sensitivity to scrapping rates applies to developed and developing markets alike, although for different reasons. In the developed markets, where replacement demand accounts for upwards of 80 per cent of total demand and scrapping rates are typically around 7-8 per cent, a one percentage point change in scrapping rates will, by definition, lead to a variation in demand of at least 11 per cent. In fact, the data in Table 3 suggest that this differential in 1990 would be as follows: EEC and OECD Oceania (11 per cent), North America (12 per cent), Other Europe (13 per cent) and Scandinavia (14 per cent).

In the developing markets, the main source of sensitivity to absolute levels of scrapping rates is not the level of replacement demand but the lowness of the scrapping rates themselves. That is, a one percentage point increase in a market where scrapping rates are 3 per cent will have a significant impact on replacement demand (i.e. a 33 per cent increase). The actual differences between the 1990 "high" and "medium" projections for the developing regions are as follows: Comecon and Africa (11 per cent), Latin America (10 per cent) and Asia (7 per cent).

The estimation of the future net impact of the various determinants of the scrapping rate is thus the critical element underlying saturation-based projections. However, this approach at least avoids the difficulty of measuring future long-term growth of incomes – a variable whose measurement is fraught with problems in periods of low growth such as at present. Moreover, scrapping rates do appear to have some predictability about them if cyclical movements are allowed for. The average lifetime of an automobile also sets an approximate upper limit to scrapping rates, and the foregoing projections have taken this factor into account to the extent possible. The next phase of the study (Chapter 3, World Supply Aspects: Technological Change) may shed further light on the likely lifetime of automobiles in the future.

Comparison with Other Agencies' Projections

Table 8 in Chapter II provides a comparison of the Secretariat's projections with those of other agencies. Taken overall, the OECD projections are in the lower half of the range. The more noticeable differences are with respect to Western Europe and Eastern Europe.

The relatively modest growth projected for Western Europe is significantly dependent on the saturation levels adopted by the Secretariat. Similarly, the relatively high estimates for 1990 provided in the Interfutures study (IFO and VDA) also appear to have been based on a saturation concept. A reconciliation of these estimates with those of the Secretariat is not immediately possible.

With respect to Eastern Europe, the Secretariat's projections are considerably lower than those of the IFO and Toyota. It is possible that the IFO projections included an income variable; in this regard it needs to be borne in mind that economic conditions prevailing in Eastern Europe at the time the projections were made (1976-77) were relatively more buoyant than they are at present.

Table 3. **Sensitivity of Secretariat's annual demand estimates
to different scrapping rates**[1]

Million units

	1985			1990			2000		
	Low	Med.	High	Low	Med.	High	Low	Med.	High
United States	10.16	11.34	12.62	10.39	11.73	13.07	11.01	12.53	14.05
Canada	0.90	1.01	1.13	0.91	1.03	1.15	1.08	1.22	1.36
North America	11.06	12.35	13.75	11.30	12.76	14.22	12.09	13.75	15.41
France	1.87	2.07	2.26	1.98	2.20	2.41	2.21	2.47	2.72
United Kingdom	1.55	1.72	1.89	1.56	1.75	1.93	1.58	1.79	1.99
Germany	2.11	2.34	2.58	2.10	2.35	2.60	2.22	2.51	2.79
Italy	1.33	1.53	1.73	1.55	1.77	2.00	1.74	2.00	2.26
Netherlands	0.48	0.53	0.58	0.51	0.56	0.62	0.56	0.62	0.69
Belgium	0.38	0.41	0.45	0.38	0.42	0.46	0.40	0.47	0.51
Denmark	0.11	0.12	0.14	0.11	0.13	0.14	0.12	0.13	0.15
Ireland	0.08	0.09	0.10	0.09	0.10	0.10	0.10	0.11	0.12
Luxembourg	0.02	0.02	0.02	0.02	0.02	0.02	0.02	0.02	0.02
Greece	0.10	0.11	0.12	0.12	0.13	0.15	0.16	0.18	0.20
EEC	8.03	8.94	9.87	8.42	9.43	10.43	9.13	10.30	11.45
Sweden	0.22	0.26	0.29	0.23	0.26	0.30	0.24	0.28	0.32
Norway	0.09	0.10	0.11	0.10	0.11	0.13	0.11	0.13	0.14
Finland	0.10	0.11	0.13	0.11	0.13	0.14	0.12	0.14	0.16
Scandinavia	0.41	0.47	0.53	0.44	0.50	0.57	0.47	0.55	0.62
Austria	0.21	0.23	0.25	0.24	0.26	0.29	0.26	0.29	0.33
Switzerland	0.25	0.26	0.27	0.24	0.26	0.29	0.27	0.29	0.32
Spain	0.65	0.75	0.84	0.63	0.75	0.87	1.07	1.22	1.37
Portugal	0.09	0.10	0.11	0.10	0.12	0.13	0.14	0.16	0.18
Turkey	0.11	0.12	0.13	0.15	0.16	0.18	0.25	0.28	0.31
Iceland	0.01	0.01	0.01	0.01	0.01	0.01	0.01	0.01	0.01
Yugoslavia	0.31	0.33	0.37	0.34	0.38	0.43	0.40	0.47	0.53
Other Europe	1.63	1.80	1.98	1.71	1.94	2.20	2.40	2.72	3.05
Japan	3.82	4.15	4.48	3.21	3.60	3.99	3.59	4.05	0.51
Australia	0.47	0.53	0.60	0.52	0.60	0.67	0.63	0.72	0.81
New Zealand	0.10	0.12	0.13	0.11	0.13	0.14	0.12	0.14	0.16
Oceania	4.39	4.80	5.21	3.84	4.33	4.80	4.34	4.91	5.48
Total OECD	25.52	28.36	31.34	25.71	28.96	32.22	28.43	32.23	36.01
USSR	1.04	1.14	1.24	1.33	1.47	1.61	2.06	2.30	2.54
Other Comecon	0.90	1.00	1.11	1.04	1.17	1.31	1.39	1.59	1.79
Total Comecon	1.94	2.14	2.35	2.37	2.64	2.92	3.45	3.89	4.33
Rep. S. Africa	0.34	0.37	0.40	0.40	0.44	0.48	0.53	0.60	0.65
Rest of Africa	0.35	0.40	0.44	0.45	0.51	0.57	0.69	0.78	0.88
Total Africa	0.69	0.77	0.84	0.85	0.95	1.05	1.23	1.38	1.53
Brazil	1.14	1.25	1.35	1.55	1.71	1.86	2.56	2.83	3.12
Argentina	0.27	0.31	0.35	0.33	0.37	0.42	0.44	0.50	0.57
Rest of South America	0.21	0.25	0.28	0.27	0.31	0.35	0.41	0.48	0.55
Mexico	0.41	0.45	0.50	0.57	0.64	0.70	1.09	1.21	1.32
Rest of Central America	0.17	0.19	0.22	0.22	0.25	0.28	0.29	0.37	0.42
Total Latin America	2.20	2.45	2.70	2.94	3.28	3.61	4.79	5.39	5.98

1. Low and high variants are based on scrapping rates set at one percentage point either side of the rates adopted.

51

Million units

	1985			1990			2000		
	Low	Med.	High	Low	Med.	High	Low	Med.	High
India	0.07	0.08	0.09	0.08	0.09	0.11	0.11	0.13	0.15
ASEAN	0.26	0.30	0.33	0.36	0.40	0.45	0.52	0.59	0.66
Rest of South East Asia	0.10	0.11	0.13	0.13	0.15	0.16	0.22	0.25	0.28
Middle South Asia	0.27	0.29	0.32	0.40	0.44	0.47	0.67	0.74	0.82
Middle East	0.63	0.66	0.68	0.83	0.87	0.90	1.26	1.33	1.39
Total Asia	1.33	1.44	1.55	1.80	1.95	2.09	2.78	3.04	3.30
Total non-OECD	6.16	6.80	7.44	7.96	8.82	9.67	12.25	13.70	15.14
Total world	31.68	35.16	38.78	33.67	37.78	41.89	40.68	45.93	51.15

1. Low and high variants are based on scrapping rates set at one percentage point either side of the rates adopted.

52

Chapter III

THE SUPPLY OF AUTOMOBILES: MAIN FACTORS INFLUENCING THE FUTURE SUPPLY AND ADJUSTMENT STRATEGIES

Chapter III will discuss some basic factors influencing the supply of automobiles and the strategies adopted to respond to these factors and to the changes in demand discussed in the previous chapter.

I. TECHNOLOGICAL CHANGE AND ITS IMPACT ON THE AUTOMOBILE INDUSTRY

In the first section of this part an analysis is made of the reasons for and types of technical change. The second section contains an assessment of the impact of these technical changes on the structure of the industry, including references to investment trends, research and development expenditures.

Section 1

FACTORS INFLUENCING TECHNICAL CHANGE IN THE INDUSTRY

There are many different factors which influence the direction of technical change in the automobile industry. In order to simplify their analysis, a broad distinction will be made here between "non-market" and "market" forces.

A. "Non-market" forces

"Non-market" forces consist mainly of government legislation or regulations of automobile use and are primarily concerned with safety and environment. Some of these regulations have affected the techological strategies of many automobile manufacturers. Given the evolving world automobile structure and the increased level of international competition, the legislation and regulations question will continue to have important consequences.

It is useful first to describe the impact of certain measures introduced in the United States, since they have had a large impact internationally via imports. In addition, echoes of the public debate on ecology and safety in the United States were heard in the other countries with the result that safety and environmental legislation was generally tightened up following the US lead.

Towards the end of the 1960s, there was an upsurge of public interest in environmental questions. In the United States, there was concern about the level of atmospheric pollution, which was largely attributed to the excessive use of cars in congested urban areas. Similar concern about the environmental quality of life was expressed in Japan as well as in other countries. Questions were also raised concerning car safety. In particular a book by US consumer advocat Ralph Nader, entitled "Unsafe at any Speed", focused on the allegedly dangerous handling characteristics of a particular car model. In response to this public interest in car safety and atmospheric pollution, the United States government introduced legislation to deal with these problems. This was embodied in the National Highway Traffic Act of 1966 and in the 1970 Clean Air Act, which proposed a number of mandatory changes designed to make cars safer.

The implementation of new safety standards led to certain changes in the design of the product. Further changes to the product were also required to meet tougher air pollution standards. This sometimes required the development and installation of new equipment, and thus government legislation or regulations can be said to have induced a number of product innovations.

The impact of these measures on the US automobile industry was not neutral. Owing to their different sizes and different levels of financial strength, some American companies were able to finance these additional costs more easily than others. Company size is a factor in the ability to finance these additions since larger firms can benefit from economies of scale in producing safety and anti-pollution equipment assuming no co-operation exists among them. Companies' ability to recoup these costs, which for the purpose of analysis can be treated as fixed costs, thus varies with the volume of sales[1]. In the light of the subsequent difficulties of the United States industry, the impact of new, more stringent standards should not be overlooked.

Between 1967 and 1973 there was a substantial (around 20 per cent) decline in the fuel economy of American cars. New safety requirements led the manufacturers to incorporate additional, weighty, equipment; and the exhaust emission control devices used to comply with the environmental regulations reduced the overall fuel efficiency of the engines. Since 1975 however, with the introduction of the catalytic converter, the fuel efficiency of the engines has been greatly improved.

These factors have evidently influenced the international competitive position of the United States industry. The other international manufacturers, whose cars were by and large more fuel-economical, were in a much better competitive position when the time came for increases in the energy price. It is perhaps significant also that the technical solutions adopted by the manufacturers to cope with the regulations in the United States were based on the continuation of domestic fuel prices below the world price level.

A new approach to the regulatory question has recently been developed in the United States. As part of a Government-wide regulatory review process, those Federal agencies which regulate the automobile industry are continuously weeding out those rules which can no longer show a net benefit. Similar examination is applied to any proposed new regulations. In the future, the burden of unnecessary regulations will be minimised and the manufacturers will be more able to use their own innovative thinking in designing cars to meet market demands[2].

Other countries also subjected their industry to new regulations of varying stringency. In Japan, the environmental and pollution requirements were at least equally severe as those applied to cars in the United States. (The application of the 1978

---

1. For further comments on this point, see the Harbridge House Report, *Corporate strategies of the Automative Manufacturers* in the Hearings of the Senate Committee on Banking, Housing and Urban Affairs, 26th April 1979, page 23.
2. *The United States Automobile Industry,* Report to Congress from the Secretary of Transportation (1981).

automobile exhaust regulation was delayed for some time in the case of imported cars in application of the government efforts to simplify import procedures.)

Japanese manufacturers' voluntary targets for fuel consumption also influenced the competitive position of the industry by furthering appropriate technical changes.

In Europe, safety regulations are generally rather stringent; those regarding environment (except noise) are less so. As in Japan, producers have generally adopted voluntary commitments concerning fuel consumption. The very different legislation concerning environment and safety in the European countries makes it difficult to adopt the common European strategy which seems to be needed from the industrial structure point of view. Rising fuel prices have led all producers rapidly to implement new technology to reduce fuel consumption of their vehicles.

B. Market Forces

The considerable oil price increases in 1973 and 1979 have caused large increases in the real price of gasoline. In the short run, this has generally led to a reduction in the number of kilometres driven, as explained in Chapter II of this report. Recently, the costs of owning a car have also been increased by high interest rates which have raised the cost of borrowing money to finance new car purchases. This has tended to some extent to reduce the demand for new cars.

In most OECD countries, the increased costs of imported oil have been passed on more or less completely to the consumer as higher real gasoline prices, which in turn have stimulated manufacturers and consumers to adjust their behaviour. The medium-term reaction of most producers was to produce more fuel-efficient cars (see Table 15). These changes were largely introduced by manufacturers trying to sustain the demand for new cars; in the United States, a direct legislative approach (the 1975 Energy Policy and Conservation Act) was also adopted in the absence of effective market signals from the gasoline refining industry, where fuel prices were much lower than the world average.

Table 15. **Improvements in fuel efficiency of new cars**
Gasoline consumption in litre/100 km

	1978	1979	1980	1985 targets
Australia	11.8	11.2	10.2	8.5
Canada	13.1	12.4	11.8	8.6
F.R. Germany	9.6	9.4	9.0	8.1-8.6
Italy[1]			(8.3)	(7.5)
Japan		8.6	8.3	7.8
Sweden		9.2	9.0	8.3
United Kingdom	10.0	9.9	9.6	8.4
United States	13.1	12.4	11.8	8.6

1. For Italy, the figures represent the average efficiency of the total car fleet.
Source : International Energy Agency, 1981.

C. The Consequences

Under the pressure of the factors described above, the automobile industry will have substantially to rethink many features of the automobile, to maintain performance and reduce costs. This rethinking involves, among other things, incorporating technologies such as electronics, or increasing the use of non-ferrous materials, and will lead to an overall rise in the technical standards used. Such design variables as fuel economy and weight will continue to have much greater importance than they did a few years ago.

These developments suggest that the automobile industry will continue to experience a period of more rapid technical change and a new period of development where the basic parameters of the social and economic situation have also changed.

Technical change is traditionally divided into two areas: product and process innovations. They will both be discussed briefly, and some assessment of their influence on competitive behaviour will be made.

D. Product Innovation

The main stimulus for product innovations comes from the urgent necessity of reducing vehicle fuel consumption. High fuel prices in all OECD countries have led to changes in consumer behaviour. Consumers are in the short run interested in maintaining existing patterns of vehicle use, but in reducing their costs. This can be done by switching to smaller cars, or by reducing current fuel consumption levels to the point where, for example, total consumer expenditure on fuel is similar to what it was pre-1973, while kilometres driven remain about the same. This implies a large increase in the mechanical efficiency of automobiles.

Consider the following pre-1973 situation. Assuming that 15 000 km are driven each year in a car that consumed ten litres per 100 km, when the petrol price was, say, DM.0.7 per litre, then the car owner would have spent DM.1 050 per year on fuel. If the amount driven and the total expenditure on fuel are to remain the same, while the fuel price increases to DM.1.50 per litre, then fuel consumption has to improve to 4.6 litres per 100 kilometres, simply to maintain consumer expenditures on fuel at pre-1973 levels. Most manufacturers are aiming at such long-term consumption figures. However, in the event that prices rise above DM.1.50 per litre it would appear that consumer expenditures on fuel would have to rise permanently, despite the impact of fuel-saving technology. The consequences of this will be discussed later.

Fuel consumption can be reduced in two ways. These are:

a) increasing the power gained from a given amount of fuel and
b) decreasing body weight and wind resistance, so the power that is produced is used more effectively.

Both of these approaches involve additional costs. The consumer is therefore very probably going to have to face the choice of higher initial capital cost for a car in return for a lower running cost. One estimate of these savings was given by Volkswagen. On the assumption that petrol costs DM.2.00 per litre, then a saving of 1 litre per 100 kilometres driven will save the owner approximately DM.3 000 over the lifetime of a car. It can be expected, therefore, that a consumer would be willing to pay up to the present value of DM.3 000 for his more efficient car, but no more. The question is whether such changes can be embodied in a car for that amount of money, or for less.

The following remarks are only indicative of some of the more important technological changes and developments which are sources of improved efficiency.

Increased Compression Ratios in Petrol Engines

This increases the power/weight ratio of the engine, so that, for a given output, energy inputs can be reduced. The principal advantage of this approach is that it requires re-designing only a new cylinder head for the engine. This can be made compatible with existing engine designs. The production technology is known and is compatible with existing lines of transfer machinery. Further, the new design is only slightly more expensive than those currently in use.

Work is also being conducted on a so-called "fireball" principle, where changes are made in the combustion chamber so that the mixture is more completely burned. It has been estimated that a fuel saving of up to 20 per cent could be thus obtained[3].

There are several disadvantages to such an approach. Increasing compression ratios tend to increase the hydrocarbon emissions, and thus add to atmospheric pollution. Higher compression ratios are easier to obtain with leaded fuel, which causes environmental problems. Higher octane fuel can be obtained without using lead, but it is likely to be more expensive.

Increased compression ratios lead to higher engine operating temperatures, and thus require improved cooling systems. Other components may wear out more rapidly at higher temperatures, thus reducing the effective lifetime of the engine. Generally speaking, an overall improvement of fuel economy of up to 5 per cent could be expected using this approach.

Improvements in Combustion

Improvements can be achieved in several ways. Lean combustion engines can be used, which give appreciable savings on inter-city driving. However, they require more exact ignition systems. This can be obtained if fuel injection systems are used. Several are being developed, or are available. They vary in design between those adjusting the mixture to the quantities of air, or to the quantity of petrol that has been pre-set. They can produce overall savings of up to 10 per cent, and also lead to increases in engine performance and reduced exhaust emissions. Further developments could be expected, so that optimal performance can be achieved with respect to load, temperature and other factors. They cost between 10 and 15 per cent more than conventional carburettors. A further feature of such systems is that they also adjust to the wear and tear of the car, so that they continue to give optimal performance even as the car ages.

Further changes can be obtained from using exhaust-driven turbo-chargers. They increase engine performance so that current performance levels could be maintained using smaller engines. Fuel savings of between 5 and 15 per cent have been reported. Their chief disadvantage is that an exhaust system of a turbo driven car could cost about twice that of a normal system.

Improvements to the Diesel Engine

In recent years there has been a notable increase in the sale of diesel-powered cars. Their main advantage lies in their lower fuel consumption and greater durability. Current levels of fuel consumption in diesels can be improved by using direct fuel injection. Savings on current diesel consumption levels, which are already as much as 25 per cent lower than equivalent petrol driven engines, can be between 10 per cent and 25 per cent, depending on whether direct or indirect injection methods are used.

Diesels are heavier and cost more than equivalent petrol driven engines. A diesel derivative of a petrol driven engine costs about 20 to 25 per cent more, while a new diesel engine costs about 50 per cent more than its petrol engine equivalent.

The increase in diesel fuel consumption could also involve supply problems. Current oil-cracking technology produces certain yields of different fuels for a given input of crude oil. These proportions can be changed, but it is expensive to do so. Greater proportions of diesel fuel also produce unwanted by-products in the refinery. There may be de facto limits set by refining capacity on how much diesel may be obtained from crude oil.

3.   *The Economist*, July 1981.

A related question is that of price policy for diesel fuels. In some countries, there is a tax preference for automotive diesel fuel. If refining costs are higher, and final prices the same or lower than for petrol, then profit margins will be correspondingly less. However, most countries do not have well-defined policies in this area.

Improvements to Transmission (and power train)

Many new models feature front-wheel drive and transmissions, where the engines are mounted transversely. This allows a more efficient use of space, thus permitting a shrinking of the outside dimensions of a car, without sacrificing passenger room. This has the benefit of reducing the overall weight of the car.

There is some evidence that the front-wheel drive configuration is more expensive to produce than its rear-wheel drive predecessor, which would tend to increase final prices. The main area for new application of this technology is North America, since many firms in Europe and Japan adopted this technique several years ago.

Further developments of the transmission are likely, including five or more speed gear boxes, and more extensive use of automatic transmissions. Some experts consider that the more widespread use of a variable speed gear box is likely, where the engine runs at its optimal speed all the time. It would appear likely that changes in transmission design, while reducing fuel consumption, will also (as is the case with most technological improvements) add to the final price of the vehicle.

Changes to the Car Body

Improved efficiency via changes in the car body can be achieved two ways. The first involves improving the aerodynamics of the car, and so reducing the amount of wind resistance and drag. Between 1968 and 1976 the average amount of wind resistance (expressed by the drag coefficient C_d) was 0.46. During this time only seven car models had a C_d value of less than 0.4. The significance of these figures can be seen when it is realised that a reduction of the C_d value from 0.5 to 0.3, a 40 per cent reduction, will lead to a 33 per cent reduction in fuel consumption when the vehicle is travelling at a constant 150 km/h. This gives some idea of the upper limit of fuel savings available as a result of aerodynamic improvements.

It has been estimated that with relatively small changes in the design of the front bumper and the front of the car the C_d value of the average saloon car could be reduced by some 13 per cent, which in turn could lead to a 9 per cent cut in fuel consumtion at high speeds[4]. Additional small changes in the design of the rear roof pillars could reduce the C_d value by a further 3 to 4 per cent. However, such changes are of a one-off variety: in the future further marginal reductions in wind resistance for instance may cost too much to be economical.

The advantage of this approach is that relatively small changes to body components can produce disproportionately large changes in fuel consumption. These changes can be incorporated in style changes considered necessary for marketing purposes.

Extensive re-styling along more aerodynamically efficient lines requires long production runs to be worthwhile. This suggests that the mass volume producers may adopt this approach sooner than the specialist producers do.

The second approach involves taking weight out of the car body and engine. The best example of this process in action was the "down-sizing" of American cars: the external dimensions of the car were reduced, while leaving the size of the passenger compartment and engine unchanged.

4. Kleinstuber D. (1979), p. 258-259.

Another possibility is to substitute other materials for steel and to substitute lighter, more durable steels than those currently used. While light metals, alloys and plastics have desirable technical properties, they tend to be more expensive than the materials they replace. In addition, problems with the manufacturing process still have to be resolved. This suggests that a steady substitution of existing parts will take place rather than a rapid jump to a car using fundamentally different materials.

Steel

As Table 16 shows, there has been a shift in the last few years away from ordinary carbon steel towards high strength steel. This substitution permits less steel to be used in carrying a given load and so reduces body weight. High strength steel is used mainly in the bumpers, wheel discs and rims, and in the load-bearing struts on the body/chassis unit. Some 50-70 kg of high strength steel are used in an average Japanese car, and that figure is expected to double during the 1990s. Similar developments are expected for European and American cars. Changes are also expected in the type of steel sheets used: owing to its anti-corrosion properties, more zinc-treated and pre-coated steel sheet is likely to be used in the future. It is likely also that a higher proportion of alloy steels will be used for engines, transmissions and chassis parts. Improvements in fatigue and wear resistance have been obtained using low carbon chrome-aluminium and chrome-titanium steel alloys.

These changes in the type of steel used in the automobile industry demonstrate a shift towards higher value steels of better quality. This suggests that, while less steel will be used overall, it will be of a higher value, and will be produced according to more exact specifications.

Table 16. **Materials consumption for a typical US car**

Figures refer to % weight

Materials	1976	1979	%
High strength steel	3.1	4.4	41.9
Aluminium	2.2	3.7	6.8
Plastics	4.3	5.5	27.9
Glass	2.3	2.4	4.3
Copper	0.85	0.81	−4.7
Zinc	1.17	0.78	−33.0
Rubber	4.0	4.1	2.5
Lead	0.66	0.69	4.5
Stainless steel	0.76	0.74	−2.6
Iron	14.9	14.2	−4.6
Plain carbon steel	55.1	52.5	6.0
Other alloys, cloth, cardboard, etc.	5.2	4.4	−15.3
Total weight lbs	3 760	3 452	−8.19

Source : U.S. Sub-Committee on Trade. Ways and Means Committee, House of Representatives, 1980.

Alloys and Aluminium

These are mainly used for load-bearing surfaces. The use of light metals permits lighter bodies while maintaining the necessary structural strength and rigidity. It has been estimated that 1 kg of aluminium can substitute for about 3.2 kg of steel, which suggests that weight savings of between 50 and 70 per cent are possible when aluminium components are used.

59

Other studies have shown that up to 72 kg could be saved in a standard Volkswagen Golf. The largest saving comes from using more aluminium (45 per cent), the second largest saving arises from using alloys and special steels (35 per cent) and the remaining 20 per cent of the 72 kg comes from using more plastic[5]. Other studies suggest that engine weight could be reduced by nearly half by converting to aluminium, and that body weight could be reduced by up to 30 per cent by using more plastic[6].

The main advantage of using such materials is that they are light and often corrosion resistant. However, apart from the greater expense, there are problems involved with the machining and preparation of such special metals. This can require more expensive processing and slower rates of production. While value productivity might rise, physical productivity would probably fall. The main result is that car prices would rise when more non-ferrous materials are used.

Plastics

As can be seen from Table 16, the use of plastics in American cars has increased considerably. The advantage of plastic components is their reduced weight and their noise dampening effects. In addition plastics do not suffer from corrosion and are easy to repair after collisions. It is also possible to make complicated forms and shapes fairly easily.

There are several different types of plastic, and their use is to some extent determined not only by cost and styling factors, but also by local safety regulations. While the overall amount of plastic used in Japanese and American cars is similar, the types of plastic differ markedly. The proportion of polyurethane used in safety equipment such as bumpers and outer body panels is higher in the United States than in Japan. A higher proportion of Fibre Reinforced Plastic (FRP) is used in American than in Japanese cars. FRP plastic can be used for the front and rear ends of cars and for the headlamp clusters. PVC type plastic forms a higher proportion of plastics used in the Japanese industry, where it is used for interior trim, seats, instruments panels and for some exterior parts such as roof linings. It is expected that future growth in plastics will tend to be concentrated more in polypropylene, polyethylene and FRP type plastics than in PVC[7].

Further developments can be expected using metal-plastic "sandwiches" which combine the lightness and corrosion resistance of plastic with the tensile strength of metal.

The principal difficulties associated with using plastics are that they are generally more expensive than metal parts and frequently cannot be used to carry heavy loads. In addition, difficulties have been experienced with the rate of moulding cycles, their "paintability", and with reliable methods of joining the plastic to metal, such that reasonably comprehensive performance guarantees can be met at acceptable costs. Problems have also been experienced with carbon fibres. A cheap high grade reliable fibre material suitable for mass production at current industry volumes has yet to be found.

The lighter materials which can replace steel components in automobiles tend to be expensive, which means the question of waste scrap metal becomes more important. Non-ferrous metals and alloys are both more difficult to cast and machine. One method of overcoming these disadvantages is to change the manufacturing process. There have been recent developments in metal powder technology, the powders being more expensive than ordinary metal, but lighter and stronger. Pressure-forming lowers scrap

5. Hildebrandt, C. H. (1980).
6. Wilkens, R. (1980), Daimler Benz (1979), pp. 594-596 and Heyl, G. (1980), pp. 18-20.
7. M. Osawa and M. Ide, *Trends of automaterials in Japan*, M.I.T., Hakone, 1982.

rates and improves tolerances so that the components require less machining. In some cases, this may lead to lower component costs.

Other New Materials

There is a trend towards the increased application of ceramic materials to engines. They have the advantage of being cheaper to use than metals or alloys; while offering some of the advantages of lightness, durability, and corrosion resistance. They also permit further improvements of engine performance since they can withstand higher operating temperatures.

Electronics

This is an area where major developments are likely to occur over the next 10-15 years, and where the range of services embodied in a car is likely to increase. The inception of electronics in manufacturing industries and in automobiles would warrant a study in itself. The few comments hereunder only intend to give some insight into the possibilities and consequences for the automobile industry[8]. Up until now, all the changes in the product which have been considered have ultimately been concerned with the question of how the existing design specifications can be carried out more efficiently. The extended application of electronics to cars will increase driving performance and safety, as well as adding to passenger comfort in ways which will considerably change the sort of services currently expected of a car.

The impact of such technological change on the automobile industry structure is likely to be large, and the influence of public measures or policies in determining electronics-related design and reliability specifications is considerable.

The structure of demand for electronic systems in cars for 1978, together with an estimate of future demand patterns (1988) is presented in Table 17. At the moment, American and Japanese cars contain more electronic components on average than their European counterparts. Expenditures on electronic systems amount to FFrs.240 per car in Europe compared to Frs.600 for American and Japanese models[9]. At the end of the 1970s, the automobile industry accounted for about 4 per cent of the world demand for semi-conductors .

As can be seen in Table 17, it is estimated that this will change during the 1980s. In 1978, the bulk of electronics used in a car were applied to engine and electronic control devices. These include devices for regulating fuel carburation, exhaust emissions, as well as for speed controls and for alternators/regulators. In the United States, these accounted for over three-quarters of all electronic systems installed in 1978, and for over half in Japan and Europe. It can be appreciated that the rate and type of application of electronic systems is heavily influenced by environmental and safety regulations and by the price of fuel.

The other areas of application expected to show rapid growth in the 1980s are safety systems, passenger comfort and driving aids. Driving aids and electronic instrumentation already account for one third of the systems used in Europe and Japan, and the forecast, which is conservative, is that this proportion will not change. Much more rapid growth is expected in safety systems, which are also influenced by public policy. The two main areas of current interest are in passive passenger restraints and in anti-locking braking systems. The latter are not yet legally required but, given technological developments and consequent price reductions, could become so in the future.

8. See also Appendix B of the report.
9. CREI, Lettre 2000, May 1981, Paris.

Table 17. **Structure of demand for electronic systems in automobiles**

In percentage

		Total amount spent Frs. millions	Engine control devices[1]	Electric control devices[2]	Safety systems[3]	Passenger comfort[4]	Driving aids instrumentation[5]
Europe	1978	2 336	31	24	0.4	2.7	39
	1988	9 827	29	12	7.1	15.3	35
USA	1978	5 728	59	19	0.1	12.2	9.0
	1988	19 346	35	6	19.3	18.7	19.8
Japan	1978	3 636	38	19	0.3	11.0	30
	1988	10 085	37	8	4.3	18.6	31

Definitions :

1. Engine control devices :
   - carburettors
   - fuel injection
   - exhaust emission
   - speed control
   - transmission
2. Electric control devices :
   - alternator
   - régulator
   - other electric systems

3. Safety :
   - suspension
   - anti-skid systems
   - passive passenger restraint
4. Comfort :
   - air conditioning
   - seat position
   - door controls

5. Driving aids :
   - dash board instrumentation
   - gauges
   - warning devices
   - speedometer

Source : CREI - Table 2, Paris, 1981.

The main drawbacks limiting the further application of electronics are the costs and the reliability of the equipment. The latter is especially important. While certain electronic components, such as speedometers, are of relatively simple design based on mechanical principles, and are extremely reliable, others are very sophisticated, costly, and may be more subject to error. Numerous technical possibilities exist where the overall efficiency gains might be too small to make it worthwhile installing them. This is particularly so with sensitive electronic components which have to survive in the extremely demanding physical environment presented by the car. Automobiles represent, in the opinion of some manufacturers, the next harshest operating environment after the military combat environment.

A further issue is whether different components in the car should be made more "intelligent" by adding micro-processors to them, or whether the micro-processor should be centralised into a vehicle computer. The latter possibility suggests further link-ups with central computer controlled traffic guidance systems which would allow more optimal use of road space. However, these developments lie years in the future.

Alternative Fuels

Further product changes have occurred by adapting petrol engines to run on other fuels such as alcohol, electricity or Liquefied Petroleum Gas. LPG share in fuel use in cars has for example been estimated at 3 per cent in 1981 and could increase to 5 per cent by 1990. However, with the exception of Brazil, and to a lesser extent Argentina and New Zealand, no country has yet decided on a large-scale switch away from petrol and diesel fuel.

The adaptation of petrol engines to alternative fuels has been done with two goals in mind. The first is to develop a fuel mixture which the engine can use more efficiently. Thus, more power can be obtained from a given volume of fuel than from the same volume of petrol. Since less fuel is consumed, consumption per kilometre falls. So long as the saving in consumption outweighs the additional cost of the new fuel, it becomes economic to use.

A second goal is to switch to cheaper fuels with lower heat content. In this case, it is economic to use the lower efficiency fuel if the savings through lower unit costs exceed the greater expenditure caused by higher consumption per kilometre.

The two main alternative fuels used are M 15, a mixture of 15 per cent methanol and 85 per cent petrol, and ethanol-petrol mixtures of up to 20 per cent ethanol and 80 per cent petrol. Fuel savings of up to 6 per cent have been reported when M 15 is used. Ethanol-petrol mixtures have been used in Brazil, and when a 10:90 mixture is used, fuel consumption per kilometre is less than for pure petroleum fuels. The use of the fuel mixtures raises the knocking resistance, and so permits higher compression ratios which raise the mechanical efficiency of the engine[10].

The main advantages of these alternative fuels is that in some countries they are cheaper than petrol, and can be used with relatively small modifications to the vehicle. The main disadvantages are the corrosive properties of methanol which requires a fuel system made of different materials. The more extended use of alcohol fuels would increase the output of hydrocarbon emissions into the atmosphere, and so cause a deterioration of the environment.

The ultimate cost saving to the consumer and to nations depends on the relative prices of petrol and alcohol fuels. These prices are determined not only by the price of production, but also by the rate of tax assessed on them. In the event that lower tax rates were levied on them, their use could become much more attractive. An increase in the range of fuels offered would require some infrastructure investment to ensure an adequate supply in all regions.

Development work has also been carried out on the use of vehicles using electricity as an alternative fuel. In some respects the more widespread use of electric vehicles would represent a switch to a new type of vehicle rather than representing a product innovation of an existing type, as is the case with the other application of alternative fuels.

The advantage of the electric vehicles is that they are non-polluting, quiet, and reasonably efficient over short distances. In many respects they appear suitable for short journeys within cities. However, electric vehicles also suffer from a number of disadvantages, some of which do not appear to be easily surmountable and look likely to limit their use during the next decade. Their chief disadvantage is their short driving range and the fairly rapid depreciation of their batteries. Battery development appears to be the main bottle-neck holding up wider use of electric vehicles.

On the assumption that the current patterns of vehicle use remain the same, the greater flexibility of petrol engines suggests that they will continue to be the dominant means of traction for the next 20 years. In the event that either oil shortages or pollution problems in city areas reach severe proportions, the use of electric vehicles would become more attractive. It might require segregation of petrol-driven inter-city traffic from intra-city traffic.

E. Process Innovation

Technological change has also affected the automobile industry in the area of process innovations. The primary motivation has been to reduce manufacturing costs. The main sources of cost savings are in reducing labour costs by using more capital and in saving material inputs by improved product design and better inventory control.

Information about these changes is relatively limited and has been mostly concerned with the impact of robots on the car assembly process. However, the kinds of

---

10. Stumpf, H.E., *Brazilian Research on Ethyl Alcohol as an Automotive Fuel in Alcohol Fuels*, August 1978, Sydney.

process innovations that are possible are closely associated with the kinds of materials used in car manufacture. As soon as plastics, composite metals and alloys are included in automobiles to a much greater extent than is usual today, it becomes difficult to infer future changes from past experience. The same is true for the application of electronics to automobiles, which could lead to major savings of material inputs and increase in end product performance by using an entirely different technology in the production of cars.

The transitional costs associated with such technical changes should be borne in mind. It is relatively easy to specify places where productivity could be improved and labour saved on the basis of existing and new methods. It is harder to predict future difficulties which might require greater concentrations of labour and capital than was formerly the case.

Annex II to this report contains a detailed examination of the use and application of robots in the automobile industry. The following paragraphs are only intended to give brief indications on trends in this area.

i) Flexible Manufacturing Systems (FMS) and Industrial Robots

The main aim of installing these systems is to reduce costs while improving the quality of the product, and so offset the cost-increasing tendencies mentioned in the previous section. The automated process systems can achieve this in a number of ways. However, before discussing these it is useful to clarify the difference between the flexible manufacturing systems (FMS) and industrial robots.

Flexible manufacturing systems consist of a line of machine tools and transfer machinery which can easily be reprogrammed to manufacture several types of components, or the same type of component to different size specifications. The emphasis here is on the "system" so that the different components operate as a combined whole.

Flexible manufacturing systems can be used, for example, in the production of engines. When applied to the casting and machining of an engine block, such systems permit one transfer line to handle the production of either six or four cylinder engines. Previously, two separate lines were necessary. The savings in fixed capital requirements are considerable.

Industrial robots, on the other hand, are devices with a degree of mobility so that by using artificial limbs, welding or other equipment can be moved to where the materials are so that the required tasks can be performed there. Given the current limitations of robots, work still has to be brought to then be correctly performed. In practical terms it is more beneficial, in terms of global productivity increases, to use robots and flexible manufacturing systems together.

One way in which these systems save costs is by improving the product quality, thus reducing the number of warranty claims and product re-calls; as product quality improves, so the number of quality inspectors can be reduced, thus saving labour costs.

Direct labour costs can also be reduced by replacing labour with robots, a process which has been facilitated by a number of factors. The improvement in micro-processor technology has meant that robots have become much cheaper. Since robots can work longer hours in poor working conditions, their hourly operating costs are now less than for an assembly worker. (For example, the calculated hourly cost of a robot working a 16 hour day in 1980 was £2.20 an hour. This compared to an average hourly cost of £4.00 for a British and £7.00 for an American worker[11].)

11. A. Black, 1981.

The application of more automated production processes not only increases the capital-labour ratio in a firm, but can contribute to a reduction in the capital-output ratio and so save capital for a given output level. It also increases the quality level of the product. A greater production flexibility is achieved. More models can be produced on an existing line, which ensures a higher degree of capacity utilisation. The higher flexibility also means that temporary shifts in consumer demand can be more quickly met by adjusting production schedules, which reduces expensive inventories normally held as "buffers".

The robots' programming flexibility, combined with their ability to work longer hours and in more difficult environmental conditions than human workers, suggest that considerable cost savings are available to the manufacturers. Studies by General Motors and Volkswagen have pointed out that some 95 per cent of components of a car weigh between 1.5 and 2.5 kg, thus making them suitable for robot assembly.

During the last few years there have been substantial increases in the number of robots used in the industry, and this trend is expected to continue in the future. This has led to spectacular increases in labour productivity (see Table 18) but should not cause the importance of other forms of automation and electronic control systems to be overlooked.

Table 18.   **Effects of robot assembly on productivity**

cars per worker per year

Average United Kingdom (1976)	7.6
Average Belgium (1976)	6.5
Longbridge (without robots)	16.0
Longbridge (with robots)	32.0
Japan average	45.0
Japan average (with robots)	67.0

Source :   The Economist, April 1980. p. 94. Bhaskar, 1979, p. 63 and p. 65.

In 1979 it was reported that the four biggest American companies had together installed about 500 robots. In 1981 GM reported that it already had 450 robots in operation and expected to increase this number to around 5000 by 1985. Toyota and Nissan used 400 and 700 robots respectively in 1981.

The main areas where robots are used are shown in Table 19. Most are used for spot welding, machining, press work and material handling. A higher proportion of robots in the United States is used for painting than in Japan. The pattern of robot use is likely to change during the course of the decade, with arc welding and assembly work become proportionately more important.

Tableau 19.   **Robot application fields**

Figures in % of total applications

	1980/81		1990 (estimated)
	USA	Japan	USA
Spot welding	40	30	4
Arc welding	6	6	15
Painting	10	1	8
Assembly	10	18	36
Other[1]	34	45	37

1.   Other includes : Material handling, Machining, Press.
Source :   Present state and future trend of introducing robots into the automobile industry in Japan. M. Ito, Hakone 1982, using figures from Cincinnati Milacron and JIRA.

ii) Optimum Production Volumes Using Automated Assembly Techniques

Despite many claims made for the application of robots, they have a number of characteristics which suggest that they do not represent a feasible technique for all situations.

Robots, as well as other forms of automatic equipment, work on a fixed cycle time, which for some Japanese companies is reported to be 45 seconds. It is quite difficult to alter this cycle time and so alter the speed of production. Out of a total cycle time of 45 seconds, 30 are used for the operation on the materials, and 15 seconds for moving between operations. Increases in line speed can mainly be achieved by reducing the operating part of the cycle, which means that each robot performs fewer tasks.

The implication of this is that the number of robots required increases as output increases. Above a certain output level the number of robots used has to increase, which suggests that the enterprise will experience rising marginal costs. Increases in output by shortening cycle times appear to be easier to reach using more global FMS systems.

Below a certain volume of production, robot assembly methods are cheaper since at those volumes more tasks can be performed by each robot, thus representing a more efficient use of capital equipment. At higher volumes shorter cycle times require more robots, thus raising costs. This suggests that greater cost advantages will be gained on small and medium sized production runs, where previously less automated production lines were used. The use of more automated assembly techniques will permit the production of a more varied range of components for more models, thus reducing the need for extreme component standardization. This will have an influence on the possible future structure of the industry as will be seen in the latter part of Chapter III.

Another question associated with existing robots is the state of sensor development. Robots are to all intents and purposes blind and have a very limited sense of touch. The additional costs involved in making sure that every component arrives in exactly the right place, in the right position and at the right time are such as to limit the number of tasks robots can perform for the time being. It seems thus unlikely that application of robots to final assembly, which is currently labour intensive, will occur within the next few years.

Section 2

TECHNOLOGICAL CHANGE, INVESTMENT AND PROFITABILITY

As was discussed above, there are two opposing trends at work in the industry: the trend towards product innovations which add value to the product and make it more expensive; the trend towards process innovations which reduce costs and so make the product cheaper. The technological changes discussed above all require important financial resources. Recent trends in investment, profitability and research and development expenditures in the industry give some indication as to the future pattern of supply of automobiles and the current amount of resources committed to the management of the process of technical change. It is not an exaggeration to say that the success or failure in managing these changes will go a long way towards determining the future pattern of supply in the industry.

As can be seen in Table 20, which intends to give only a rough estimation of the total investments in some countries (see note to the table), four countries – the United States, Japan, FR Germany and France – account for the bulk of investment in the automobile industry. Despite its current problems, the US industry is still responsible for the largest investments when measured in absolute terms.

Given the types of changes outlined in the previous section, it is likely that automobile companies will be faced with increasing R&D expenditure in the future.

Table 20. **Investment in motor vehicle industry**

Units in US$ mill. [1]

	1976	1977	1978	1979
United States	2 311	3 605	3 605	4 051
Canada[2]	89	231	262	346[2]
Sweden	214	189	201	233
Netherlands	50	45	58	62
Japan	1 341	2 418	3 014	2 692
Italy	293	382	486	n.a.
United Kingdom	301	434	707	n.a.
France	832	1 072	n.a.	n.a.
F.R. Germany	1 198	1 747	2 583	3 462[3]

1. Figures refer to total investment in vehicle industry converted into constant 1975 prices in DM and then converted into US dollars at prevailing exchange rates.
2. Figures for Canada refer to investment in Canada in current dollars by the four major US motor companies. The figure for 1980 is $ 827 m.
3. 3 625 m in 1980.
Source : VDA, 1981.

However, these expenditures, like those of safety and environmental equipment, represent unequal commitments among the companies, depending on their size. Some emerging competitive problems can be seen in Table 21, where the amounts of investment per vehicle are shown. A question may immediately be raised about the possible future structure of the world industry if the price of new equipment rises beyond the ability of smaller companies in smaller countries to pay for it. Part III of this chapter includes an analysis of various strategies for facing this sort of problem.

Investment trends in each country are shown in Table 22. The United States, Japan, FR Germany, the United Kingdom and France have experienced the largest real increase in investment in the road vehicle industry. A clear difference can be seen between the growth in investment in the larger producing countries as compared with the stagnating investment in smaller producing countries.

A surprising feature of these investment trends is that the Japanese industry's investment performance is exceeded by other countries, notably the United States and FR Germany, whether measured in absolute terms or as investment per vehicle. One interpretation of these investment figures could be that some kind of "catching up" process is taking place, and countries other than Japan are having to invest at a faster rate so as to take into account safety, environmental and economy factors as well. Another feature of this "catching up" process is probably that in some countries proportionately more investment is required to replace old uncompetitive capital

Table 21. **Investment per vehicle at 1975 prices[1]**

Converted into US dollars

	1976	1977	1978	1979
United States	201	283	296	352
Sweden	585	664	661	658
Netherlands	584	688	764	603
Japan	171	283	325	279
Italy	184	241	294	n.a.
United Kingdom	175	253	428	n.a.
France	244	305	n.a.	n.a.
F.R. Germany	309	425	617	814[2]

1. See note 1, Table 20.
2. 934 in 1980.
Sources : VDA, 1981, OECD, Main Economic Indicators, Historical Statistics.

Table 22. **Trends in investment in the motor vehicle industry in selected countries[1]**

1976 = 100

	1976	1977	1978	1979
United States	100	156.0	165.7	175
Sweden	100	100.0	97.7	109
Netherlands	100	83.9	92.6	97.0
Japan	100	147.6	149.5	164.4
Italy	100	129.8	157.1	n.a.
United Kingdom	100	129.8	196.3	n.a.
France	100	121.9	n.a.	n.a.
F.R. Germany	100	129.5	166.8	211[2]

1. Local currency 1975 prices.
2. 250 in 1980.
Source : VDA, OECD and Secretariat's calculations.

vintages, and so bring the age structure of capital equipment up to date with that of competitors. This can be understood as a remedy for years of under-investment, and may be applicable to the situation in the American and British automobile industries.

The real increases in investment over the last decade have imposed additional burdens on the industry. A summary of the profitability of some of the leading manufacturers in the automobile industry is presented below in Tables 23 and 24. The overall trend of profitability for this group of firms is slightly downwards, but there are considerable differences within the group which could influence the future pattern of supply of automobiles. As measured as a percentage of sales, net profits for the group as a whole range from 4 per cent for firms like GM or Toyota, to 1 per cent or less for a few others, which suggests that overall industry profitability is low.

The national differences in profitability are also shown in Table 24. Within the selected group of companies those from Japan were the most profitable judging the low standard deviation value. The American companies were the next most profitable over this period[12] although with much greater variability than the Japanese companies. This could suggest that many "medium-sized" companies in the United States, Japan and Europe may be confronted in the coming years with the most serious difficulties in financing the new investment required for the new generations of automobiles.

Failure to invest on a large enough scale in the industry has a number of cumulative effects which are felt over a number of years. As investment requirements for the new models increase, so insufficient financial resources lead to a slowdown in the rate of model replacement. This can adversely affect a firm's overall competitive performance against firms producing new models more rapidly. Ageing model ranges and declining sales depress profitability and make the further accumulation of investment funds more difficult.

This would suggest that a continuing careful analysis of investment plans in the automobile industry (both realised and proposed) would provide some indication of the future structure of the industry and help to foresee any longer term trade or social problems likely to occur.

Research and Development

As was pointed out above, there is increased pressure on the companies to become involved in product and process innovations. There has been increased government awareness of this issue and of its significance in the competitive process.

12. Chrysler and American Motors data was not available for inclusion.

Table 23. Net return on sales
Net profit as a percentage of sales

	1971	1972	1973	1974	1975	1976	1977	1978	1979	1980	1981
Honda	2.9	3.0	3.2	2.7	1.1	1.5	2.9	2.7	1.3	2.1	5.4
Nissan	3.4	4.1	3.3	1.3	2.9	4.2	3.6	2.8	3.2	2.8	
Toyota	3.8	4.2	5.5	2.9	2.7	5.0	5.1	4.4	3.6	4.3	
Japan average	3.4	3.8	4.0	2.3	2.23	3.56	3.8	3.3	2.7	3.0	
VW	0.9	1.3	1.9	(−4.8)	(−0.8)	4.1	1.7	2.1	2.2	1.0	
Daimler-Benz	2.1	2.5	2.2	2.0	1.9	2.1	2.2	2.3	2.3	2.1	
BMW		4.0	3.6	1.7	2.3	2.9	2.5	2.5	2.7	2.3	1.9
Opel							3.7	4.3	3.8	0.5	(−5.9)
Ford		2.8	4.1	−3.5	4.4	7.3	5.7	5.2	4.4	(−5.3)	1.4
F.R. Germany average	1.5	3.3	2.2	−1.15	1.95	4.1	3.16	3.2	3.0	0.12	
GM	6.8	7.1	6.7	3.0	3.5	6.2	6.1	5.5	4.4	(−1.3)	0.5
Ford	4.0	4.3	3.9	1.4	1.3	3.4	4.4	3.7	2.7	(−4.2)	(−2.8)
US average	5.4	3.7	5.3	2.2	2.4	4.8	5.25	4.6	3.5	−2.75	−1.15
Peugeot						4.1	3.0	2.0	1.5	(−2.1)	(−2.8)
Volvo		2.4	2.7	1.0	0.1	0.4	1.2	1.6	1.8	0.2	1.5
British Leyland							(−0.3)	0.0	(−4.1)	(−13.8)	(−12.0)
Other average	n.d.	n.d.	n.d.	n.d.	n.d.	2.25	1.3	1.2	(−0.26)	(−5.2)	(−4.4)
Overall average	3.41	3.57	3.71	0.77	1.94	3.75	3.21	3.0	2.29	−0.87	
Standard deviation	1.83	1.57	1.46	2.69	1.56	2.01	1.83	1.55	2.17	4.77	

Notes :
- Profitability is defined as profits net of taxes, interest and dividend payments. Sales represents turnover for the whole company.
- A time trend regression if the profit figures from 1971-1981 yielded the following results

$$y = 504 - 0.253T \quad r^2 = 0.51 \text{ (see Table 24).}$$

Sources : Company Annual Reports.

Table 24.   **Net return on sales by selected companies**
1971 - 80/81

	Average	Standard deviation
Honda	2.6	1.18
Nissan	3.2	0.85
Toyota	4.1	0.92
Average Japan	3.2	0.63
VW	0.96	2.36
Daimler-Benz	2.17	0.17
BMW	2.64	0.71
Opel	1.28	4.28
Ford	2.65	4.05
Average F.R. Germany	2.13	1.63
General Motors	4.4	2.75
Ford	2.0	2.93
Average USA	3.0	2.71
Peugeot	1.88	2.14
Volvo	1.21	0.65
British Leyland	−6.04	6.49
« Other » average	−0.98	3.09

Source : See Table 23.

As investment has increased, there has been a similar increase in research and development expenditure in real terms. This suggests that competition is increasingly taking place between firms in the laboratory and on the test track in the automobile industry. The main trends in R&D spending are shown in Table 25.

The effects of this expenditure are not easy to judge, since the correlation between industry success and heavy research and development expenditure is not very high. When compared internationally, the US industry has spent most on R&D. It accounted for nearly half of all research and development in the major producing countries in 1977. The relative share of the US R&D expenditure in the industry has been falling. This is largely due to the higher rate of growth in R&D expenditure by countries like Japan and France. R&D expenditure in FR Germany also increased between 1967 and 1977 but less so than in Japan, with the result that Germany is now the third largest consumer of R&D resources in the car industry. When measured on a per vehicle basis, however, FR Germany still has the highest R&D expenditure in the industry, in addition to having the highest per vehicle investment expenditure.

The implications of these trends are hard to judge. The extreme situation is represented by the United Kingdom with falling real levels of R&D. This undoubtedly makes the development of new technologies more difficult, but bearing in mind that the UK industry pioneered front-wheel drive cars with transversely mounted engines, perhaps the need for product innovations has been somewhat less than in other countries. Conversely, high R&D expenditure in the United States may have been largely absorbed by meeting emission and safety standards rather than being spent on more commercially productive innovations.

Table 25 also reveals that while R&D was of growing importance, it was privately rather than publicly financed. This suggests that the role of government in supporting motor vehicle research has been rather small, and of little competitive significance. The industry which benefited the most from public R&D expenditure was the American,

Table 25. **Research and development expenditure in motor vehicles**

R & D expenditure in constant prices ($ m)[1]

	1967	1969	1971	1973	1975	1977
USA[3]	1 151	1 621	1 631	2 209	1 789	2 173
Japan	234	325	476	674	654	812
F.R. Germany	419	626	751	621	623	751
France	201	244	313	373	361	443
Italy[2]	147	175	244	262	262	265
UK[4]	205	210	199	193	192	193
Total	2 357	3 201	3 594	4 332	3 875	4 637

	Annual average change (en %)	Shares of total R & D (%)	
	1967-1977	1967	1977
USA[3]	6.6	49.0	46.9
Japan	13.2	9.9	17.5
F.R. Germany	6.0	17.8	16.2
France	8.2	8.5	9.5
Italy[2]	6.1	6.2	5.7
UK[4]	−0.6	8.7	4.2
Total	7.0	100.0	100.0

	1977 Sources of funds (%)		Government R & D expenditure ($ m)[1]
	Industry	Government	
USA[3]	96.5	3.5	76.1
Japan	99.9	0.1	0.8
F.R. Germany	98.2	1.8	13.5
France	99.2	0.8	3.5
Italy[2]	98.5	1.5	4.0
UK[4]	95.5	4.5	8.7
Total	97.7	2.3	106.6

1. $ m at 1975 prices and 1975 exchange rates.
2. Italy also includes motor cycles, shipbuilding and railways.
3. USA by product rather than industry ; the latter would have raised the 1977 figure to $ 2 978 m, of which $ 372 m was government funded R & D not related to motor vehicles but performed by companies in the motor vehicle industry.
4. UK data adjusted for comparable years.
   Sources : Jones, D., (1982), using figures from : *OECD, Surveys of Resources Devoted to R & D by OECD Member Countries.*
Business Enterprise Sector Volumes, Paris, various years.
National Science Foundation, *Research and Development in Industry,* Washington, various years.
UN, *Yearbook of Industrial Statistics,* New York, various years.
EEC, *Structure and Activity of Industry,* 1975, Brussels, 1978.
HMSO, British Business and Economic Trends, London, various issues.

which had the highest share of government expenditure of total countries in 1977. The next largest donor of R&D funds in absolute terms was the German government, although it contributed a lower share of total industry R&D expenditure than the British government did to the British automobile industry.

General Remarks

This first part of Chapter III has highlighted the importance, for the future of the automobile industry in the major manufacturing regions, of technological developments in both products and manufacturing processes. Yet, while technology must be accorded the importance it clearly has in the industry's long-term development, a rapid transformation of existing structures would not seem to be imminent on this account. The introduction of technological improvements at the product level is a relatively slow process and its impact on structural adjustment is gradual. More important, however, from the structural standpoint are technological advances in manufacturing processes. Automated systems of production and the use of robots will play an increasing role in international competitiveness – at least until such time, probably by the end of the 1980s, as manufacturing processes will have reached a similar level of sophistication throughout the world.

Investment in R&D will thus be a decisive factor in the competitiveness of automobile manufacturers. Broadly speaking, the government role in this context is to create an economic and public environment in which technological development could flourish.

For instance, it is essential that public opinion as a whole and the workforce in particular should recognise that methods of manufacturing automobiles are important as a means of guaranteeing the industry's competitiveness and thus the employment it provides over the long term .

Where the commercial aspect of R&D is concerned, the industry itself is already beginning to organise its R&D efforts at the national and regional levels and, increasingly in the future, on a world scale. Currently, Europe provides the most striking examples. International research agreements would seem to be the natural development and government could well encourage co-operative endeavours, in particular by facilitating the removal of possible legal obstacles to such agreements.

Governments can also play an effective role in promoting basic research, particularly at the international level. The risks of causing distortions in trade are less likely in the case of basic research, particularly if it is carried out in a context of international co-operation.

Associating universities, firms, workers and governments in a joint endeavour to produce a policy for basic research might be a way of winning public acceptance for technological change. Similarly, research with a social aim (in the broadest sense of the term, i.e. protection of the environment, safety, etc.) could be encouraged by governments and possibly even carried out on an international scale with the co-operation of the parties concerned.

The following part of this Chapter on supply factors will deal with the location factor.

2. INDUSTRIAL LOCATION OF THE AUTOMOBILE INDUSTRY

A. The present trend in the United States and Europe

Table 26 shows the geographic distribution of production, by firm and by country, for some of the larger integrated US and European producers. Broadly speaking, the vast majority of production is located in traditional manufacturing areas, namely North America, Western Europe and Japan. Many of the other countries – such as Australia, Argentina and South Africa – to which production has been decentralised are themselves areas in which there is a long tradition (often predating World War II) of automobile manufacturing. Some trends can, however, be identified when Tables 26 and 27 (growth of international production) are combined.

There is a tendency for the "integrated" producers[13] to decentralise their production away from their home countries. Between 1970 and 1980 the share of domestic production among the large mass producers fell from around 80 per cent to under 75 per cent.

13. Integrated producers refer to those companies producing a range of cars for all market segments in large volumes.

72

Table 26. Geographical distribution of automobile production
by selected american and european car manufacturers[1]

	G.M.		Ford		Peugeot		Renault		V.W.		Fiat	
	1978	1980	1978	1980	1978	1980	1978	1980	1978	1980	1978	1980
United States	73	71.1	54.8	42.4	–	–	–	7.9	1.7	8.6	–	–
Canada	7.9	8.9	8.0	8.1	–	–	–	0.1	–	–	–	–
Brazil	2.2	3.1	2.6	3.8	–	–	–	–	22.5	18.9	7.2	11.7
Mexico	0.3	0.29	0.68	1.2	–	–	0.92	1.0	3.6	4.9	–	–
Argentina	–	–	0.75	2.3	1.2	1.5	1.8	2.8	0.76	1.2	1.5	2.4
F.R. Germany	13.2	13.7	11.6	13.6	–	–	–	–	70.1	66.3	–	–
France	–	–	–	–	80.7	82.6	81.7	72.2	–	–	–	–
Italy	–	–	–	–	–	–	–	–	–	–	90.5	85.8
United Kingdom	1.1	0.96	6.9	11.1	8.4	7.1	–	–	–	–	–	–
Spain	–	–	5.6	8.4	8.9	8.6	15.4	15.7	–	–	–	–
Benelux	–	–	5.7	6.1	–	–	–	–	–	–	–	–
Australia	1.6	1.7	2.3	2.5	–	–	–	–	–	–	–	–
South Africa	0.27	n.a.	0.68	n.a.	0.6	–	–	–	1.1	n.a.	0.5	–
Total (mill.)	7 216	5 174	4 660	3 081	2 314	1 748	1 519	2 065	2 288	1 288	1 377	1 381

1. Selected manufacturers' figures show a percentage of production. Totals show total production in millions of units and do not include CKD assembly or production under license.
Source : Jones, D. 1981, 1982. Secretariat calculations.

Although there has been a decentralisation of production, this move has been directed towards a relatively small number of countries, as Table 26 shows. The chief newcomers to the group of automobile producing nations are Spain and Portugal in Europe, and Brazil and Mexico in Latin America.

Furthermore, some mass-producer firms in the traditional areas have withdrawn from foreign production because of their domestic difficulties. The best examples of this are Chrysler in the United States and British Leyland in the United Kingdom. Often in such cases, companies in difficulty have sold their foreign production facilities to other companies, so that some companies' increasing share of foreign production in fact represents no more than the transfer of existing assets from one company to another rather than the construction of new plant.

Table 27. Growth of international production

Foreign production shares

	1970	1980
General Motors	32.8	28.9
Ford	45.6	57.4
Chrysler	42.8	17.4
Volkswagen	10.5	33.7
Fiat	3.6	14.2
Peugeot	4.2	17.3
Renault	11.0	27.7
British Leyland	5.8	0

Source : D. Jones, 1982.

A rapid examination of a few specific cases highlights the role of special local factors in companies' decisions to decentralise, and helps clarify the outlines of general corporate adjustment strategies.

It can be seen, for example, that General Motor's share of domestic production remains (at 71 per cent) higher than that of its main US rivals. From that perspective, General Motors would appear to be, relatively speaking, consolidating its position on the American market, where it remains strongly entrenched.

Ford, on the other hand, has expanded its foreign production much more rapidly and extensively than GM – and, indeed, more than all of the other US mass-producers. US production now accounts for under half of Ford's total production, and Ford can probably claim to be the most "international" of all automobile companies. Countries like the UK, Spain, Brazil, Mexico, Argentina and South Africa account for higher proportions of Ford's production than of GM's. Recent developments at Ford suggest that the international trend is likely to increase in the future.

The European "integrated" producers have tended to be more concentrated in their home or regional markets. One exception to this is Volkswagen, which now ranks after Ford as the second most "international" company. In recent years, however, other European producers, especially Renault, have put more emphasis on international investment, for instance in the United States or in Latin America.

B. Present trends in Japan

Until recently, the Japanese industry has been exceptional in that domestic production has accounted for a far higher proportion of total output than was usual for American and European companies. Although the Japanese industry has experienced very rapid growth in the last few years, this has not so far led to a strategy of substituting direct foreign investment for direct exports from Japan.

There is evidence that this strategy is now changing. Honda and British Leyland recently agreed to co-operate in producing a medium-sized car, the Triumph Acclaim, in the United Kingdom. Nissan has become involved in production in Spain (Motor Iberica), in Italy (Alfa Romeo) and in the United States. Toyota has taken over British Leyland factories in Australia and opened a plant at Melbourne, and Mitsubishi is now using former Chrysler facilities in Australia.

Thus, throughout the automobile industry there is a new general tendency to increase the share of international production and serve local markets from local supply points. Decisions regarding the siting of production facilities have traditionally been among the most important made by an enterprise for promoting its future growth and expansion. Such decisions are normally made after carefully considering the corporate resources available at the time, the distribution of the enterprise's strength and activities, including the existing distribution of capacity, and its general competitive position.

Before discussing some of the factors influencing the location decision, it is useful to consider an example of decentralisation of automobile production. A study of the distribution of Ford plants in the United States and in Europe (Table 28) reveals that there is a remarkable similarity in the number of plants devoted to the production of a given component in both the United States and in Western Europe. As Table 28 shows, the most notable difference between the structure of Ford production in Europe and in the United States is that there are more chassis and transmission plants in Europe. Apart from that, there is a similar distribution of engine, body and final assembly plants in both areas. This suggests that Ford seems to regard the European market as one unit from the point of view of planning and production. It has been suggested that this European-American pattern of decentralised production could also be applied to a "world car"; a further discussion of this point can be found in a later part of this chapter.

Table 28. **Decentralised production at Ford's manufacturing plants**

By function and location

Plant function and location	Number	Location	Number
United States and Canada		**Europe**	
Engine assembly			
Ohio	4	United Kingdom	3
Ontario	3	F.R. Germany	1
Michigan	1	Spain	1
Total	8	Total	5
Body stamping and castings			
Ohio	2	United Kingdom	4
Michigan	4	F.R. Germany	2
Illinois	1	Belgium	1
New York	1	Spain	1
Ontario	2		
Total	10	Total	8
Chassis/transmission			
Indiana	1	United Kingdom	4
Michigan	3	F.R. Germany	3
Ohio	1	France	2
Total	5	Total	9
General parts			
Michigan	4	United Kingdom	5
New York	1	F.R. Germany	2
Ohio	1		
Total	6	Total	7
Final assembly			
Michigan	3	United Kingdom	4
Ohio	2	F.R. Germany	2
Ontario	2	Spain	1
Illinois	1	Belgium	1
Georgia	1	Portugal	1
California	2	Ireland	1
Missouri	2		
Kentucky	1		
New Jersey	2		
Minnesota	1		
Virginia	1		
Total	18	Total	10

Source : Black, 1981 and Ford's reports.

C. Factors affecting the Location of Production Facilities and their Relative Importance

Market size

Traditionally this has been a highly important factor in influencing investment decisions, and indeed the current distribution of automobile production shows that plants are located mainly in high income countries with relatively large internal markets.

75

Market size and plant siting decisions are closely linked because of the significant economies of scale to be achieved in the industry. A summary of these economies, presented as minimum efficient scale estimates, is shown for the past years in Table 29. As was mentioned earlier, there is a strong possibility that the minimum efficient scale of production may decrease sharply in the future.

The importance of market size as a location determinant increases according to whether the existing market is large, and whether it is likely to grow in the near future. The possible future growth of market areas adjacent or near to the market in question and the political and commercial relations in the region, are also considered.

Table 29. **Minimum efficient scale estimates**

Units in millions

| Author | Scale economies for | | | | | |
	Casting	Machining	Stamping	Assembly	One model	Whole range
Pratten (1971)	1.0	0.25	0.5	0.3	0.5	1.0
Rhys (1972)	0.2	1.0	2.0	0.4	–	2.0
White (1971)	small	0.26	0.4	0.2	0.4	0.8
Bristol University	1-2	4-1.0	0.54	0.2-0.4	0.2	1.0

Source : Bhaskar, 1979.

Industrial Technology and the Quality Level of the Industrial Infrastructure

The previous part has shown that there has been an increasing emphasis on investment and on the application of new technology to the automobile industry. This means that access to skilled professional manpower is likely to become of greater importance in influencing the location decision.

Since automobile assemblers require a large number of components, not all of which can be manufactured in-house, access to a network of efficient component-supplying firms is also important. Given recent concern over inventory levels for intermediate inputs in the assembly process, those suppliers who are reasonably closely positioned to the assemblers, or at least are connected to the assemblers by good means of communication, may have some advantage.

Other significant factors are the level of technical know-how possessed by suppliers, and the effectiveness of local research and development organisations. This type of knowledge may contribute to the competitive strength of the assembly firms located near it.

Labour relations

Two factors are important here: the quality of labour, and the organisation of industrial relations.

i) Quality of labour

There are substantial national differences regarding attitudes to work, which are based on historical, social and psychological factors. Factors such as access to education and social stratification also play a role. It is not the task of this report to elaborate on this subject.

While recent developments in process technology seem likely to reduce the skill content involved in the actual assembly process, there is a growing need for technically educated workers who can understand, service and repair complex machine tools and transfer lines. Thus, generally speaking, there is a tendency for unskilled to be replaced by more technically trained workers. This suggests that availability of such labour will become a more important factor in the future.

An indication of these trends is given for one country, the United Kingdom, in Table 30, which gives a breakdown of the labour force in the vehicle industry by occupation. The high proportion of managerial and clerical staff is most noticeable. A slight downward trend in the proportion of unskilled workers can also be seen.

Another system using a more highly skilled and trained workforce is used more and more by the vehicle assemblers. The implementation of quality circles, and a higher degree of labour participation in some production decisions affecting product quality and reliability, could lead to a more harmonious working relationship and lower labour costs. At the same time, greater flexibility of the labour force could contribute to easier and faster introduction of more productive technology in the industry.

Table 30. **Employment, by occupation,
in United Kingdom automobile industry**

	1970	1977	1980
Management/clerical Foremen	19.9	26	26.4
Skilled Workers	28.4	26.3	26.8
Unskilled	34	30.6	30.3
Other	17	12.8	12.6

Note : Managerial refers to « office workers », i.e. includes Managerial, Adminis-trative, Technical and Clerical. The figures for 1970 refer to male employees only. There was a change in occupational classification between 1972 and 1973.
Source : Department of Employment Gazette. HMSO.

ii) Industrial Relations

There are quite wide national differences in the organisation of industrial relations in the automobile industry. They range from a highly fragmented trade union structure in Britain and Japan to a highly centralised structure in the United States and FR Germany. As with the quality of labour, differences in the organisation of trade unions and employers' associations can substantially affect the ease with which agreements on wages and working conditions can be reached, and the process by which enterprise consensus can best be obtained. These tend to be important factors in any new location decision.

Labour costs evidently influence the location decision, too. Since the long-term tendency is for more capital to be substituted for labour, the apparent importance of labour cost differences between countries is likely to become less important.

Government policy considerations

Policy factors can be divided broadly into those related to the policies of local government and the political and social conditions of the location; and those related to all other factors.

In terms of local government policies, the different investment incentives offered are expected to have increased importance in the coming years. Such incentives include the long-term exemption from, or reduction of, corporate income taxes and property taxes; various forms of financial assistance; the exemption from, or reduction of, import duties on capital equipment; and government-secured, long-term loans at low interest rates. Other incentives include the provision of the requisite infrastructure around the production site. Such incentives can effectively reduce the initial investment costs of a site, as well as plant operating costs. When other economic conditions are virtually identical, favourable investment incentives play a very decisive role in location decisions.

Local content requirements also play an important role in plant location decisions. Developing nations, primarily the newly-industrialising countries, have often attached export obligations or import-export tax measures to such requirements, in order to promote the industrialisation of their own country or to stem the outflow of foreign currency. Table 31 shows the trade restrictions applied by selected non-OECD Member countries. There are signs that local content requirements may also spread to the advanced industrialised countries because of the worsening of their unemployment problems.

Another policy factor is the existence of trade barriers that obstruct market access. Among these obstacles to free trade are import prohibitions and various import regulations, such as import quotas, tariff quotas and high tariff rates which effectively limit the movement of goods. Other types of measures achieve virtually the same result: these include regulations requiring high local content ratios for the component parts of imported vehicles, or requirements for voluntary exportation.

Many non-OECD countries have adopted a number of measures to limit the imports of built-up cars, and to encourage the export of locally-produced cars and components. A list of these countries is given in Table 31.

The consistency and continuity of governmental policies, as well as the political and social stability of the country itself, figure in the risk factor of a location. While the probability of a drastic political upheaval is relatively small, the main concerns – even in the developed countries – generally are about foreign investment regulations and the consistency and continuity of governmental policies affecting the automobile industry.

Tableau 31. **Trade restrictions of selected developing countries**

Country	Trade restrictions [1]		
	Local content	Import restrictions	Export requirements
Argentina	*	*	*
Brazil	*	*	*
Chile	*	*	*
Colombia	*	*	*
Mexico	*	*	*
Péru	*	*	*
Venezuela	*	*	*
India	*	*	
Indonesia	*	*	
Iran	*	*	n.a.
Israël	*	*	*
South Korea	*	*	*
Kuwait			
Malaysia	*	*	n.a.
Pakistan	*	*	*
Philippines	*	*	*
Saudi Arabia			
Taiwan	*	*	
Thailand	*	*	
Algeria		*	
Egypt	*	*	
Libya	n.a.	n.a.	n.a.
Morocco	*	*	
Nigeria	*	*	

1. Import restrictions apply to non-tariff measures which deal solely with imports.
Source : US Congress, 1980, and SMMT, 1979, cited in D. Jones, 1981.

In the case of developing and state-trading countries, the degree of business freedom (controlling rights) that can be assured at a production location is also an important factor to assess.

Any government's policy objectives which, in a broad sense, are related to matters of national security – may also have an impact because of the automobile industry's inherent capacity to generate employment and because of its strategic and symbolic nature.

A theoretical effort to rank the most influential policy considerations for each principal region could give the following results: Advanced newly industrialising countries – investment incentives, employment demands; Industrialising countries – local content regulations, investment incentives; Developing nations – trade barriers, consistency of governmental policies; State trading countries – degree of business freedom, country risk factor.

General remarks

In the automobile industry, decisions regarding location are based on a series of economic, industrial, financial and social policy factors. Although the broad outline of a general trend in location is discernible in world-wide very long-term location policy, fluctuations in these various factors can, in the short and medium term, affect the pace and pattern of this general trend.

In the very long term, apart from the continuous process of modernisation of the industry's capital stock (primarily on the scrap-and-build basis) in the most advanced industrial countries in OECD, it would seem that most totally-new production capacities will be set up first of all in the newly industrialising countries and then, little by little, in some of what are now developing countries. This is likely to lead to some degree of specialisation amongst manufacturers and increasingly (but only in the highly industrialised countries) to the production of more sophisticated passenger cars. At the same time, a complex system of international trading links, may lead to the development of several types of "world" or "regional" cars with versions for the different markets.

In addition to the general requirements of favourable economic conditions, existing industrial bases and, more specifically, market size and the level of technological development, two additional factors should be noted: the human factor and the political factor.

In an industry which, despite the spread of automation, will continue to be labour-intensive, the quality in terms of both professional skill and reliability of the workforce is crucial. Work skills are imparted by the system of education and are thus the fruit of a long-term effort. In this respect the newly-industrialising countries are gradually approaching the level of the industrialised ones. The question of labour stability or reliability is another matter, since it involves the question of the quality of management – in other words, labour-management relations. We have seen that one key factor for the automobile industry in the future will be its ability to adapt rapidly to changing conditions in demand and technology. The most industrialised countries will, therefore, need consistently to direct their efforts in this area to finding a flexible style of social relations, steering round the rigidities engendered by several decades of almost uninterrupted growth. Governments can encourage this. This adaptability in social relations is essential if the industrialised countries are to stay in the race – particularly with the newly industrialising countries, where social relations have not reached the same degree of rigidity or maturity as in the older industrialised countries and are thus both more flexible and more adaptable.

Another factor which could have a crucial effect is government policy. Although it is clear that neither the automobile industry nor governments themselves favour intervention by the public authorities in the industry's problems, it is nonetheless also clear that government cannot fail to take an interest in an industry that is both labour-intensive and a generator of further industry. This has already led (and could continue to lead) to policy measures affecting location policy and, consequently, the future world-wide structure of the automobile industry. Such intervention has been seen, in particular, during periods of economic depression, when governments assist firms in difficulty to overcome their structural problems. But it has also been seen during more stable periods, or in periods of economic growth when governments want to encourage investment in order to maintain or promote industrialisation. It would seem important for governments, when they take such initiatives, both to comply with generally-accepted principles of positive adjustment policies and to consider the effects that their proposed course of action are likely to have on trade and on the adjustment policies of their partners. The final conclusions to the report will return to this important aspect.

3. SOME ADJUSTMENT STRATEGIES

A. Evolution of the Present System

The post war expansion of the automobile industry has been closely associated with the growth of free trade. Before the Second World War, trade barriers had led to a trade system wherein a few European countries exported to protected areas, while the US industry largely supplied the rest of the world.

In the production system that evolved during the 1950s and early 1960s, the larger OECD countries produced well over 90 per cent of the world's cars. These were produced primarily for their own domestic markets, and exports were of secondary importance. With the exception of some non-producing OECD countries, like the Benelux, imports only captured large market shares in non-OECD markets. During this period, imports took between 1 and 5 per cent of the OECD producing countries' market.

As the 1960s wore on, though, production was still primarily centred on the larger OECD countries, but there was a much higher inter-penetration of OECD markets. Imports took a much larger proportion – between 5 and 15 per cent – of domestic sales. The growth of domestic markets centred on flows within the OECD areas. This trade was mainly in finished vehicles, but exports to developing countries increasingly tended to be in the form of Completely Knocked Down (CKD) kits. This avoided certain tariff and non-tariff barriers, the geographical extent of which has been shown in Table 31.

In the late 1970s, two factors put growing pressures on this system: a growing imbalance of international trade within the OECD area (caused largely by the appearance of the Japanese industry on the world market), and the increasing reticence of the developing countries to import finished automobiles.

Before the war, the US industry had also had a considerable competitive advantage on world markets; and it is interesting to see that, partly in response to trade barriers, the American manufacturers invested overseas and established local production facilities.

The current trade system can essentially be described as a triangular flow of cars between the United States, Europe and Japan. The United States is the largest net importer of cars, absorbing vehicles from both Japan and Western Europe. It has the largest trade deficit of the three areas. Japan is the largest net exporter, sending cars to the United States and, to a lesser extent, to Western Europe and thus has the largest

Table 32. **Origin of passenger vehicle imports**

From To	EEC		Japan		USA	
	1979	1980	1979	1980	1979	1980
EEC	–	–	66.0	74.3	26.5	24.8
Japan	11.5	14.0	–	–	45.0	50.9
United States	1.6	0.7	29.6	21.7	–	–

Source : OECD, Series C, *Foreign Trade Statistics.*

trading surplus. Western Europe has the most balanced trade in cars, running a surplus with the United States and developing countries, and a deficit with Japan. The quantitative outlines of the system are shown in Table 32.

Another factor responsible for a change in the system was the growing unwillingness of developing countries to import finished cars. Instead there was a desire to harness the dynamic automobile industry to the needs of their internal industrial development. The developing countries attempted to "capture" the employment and growth benefits by instituting local content rules and export targets for domestic producers, the extent of which was illustrated above.

The combination of these factors with the product and process innovation described in a previous part of this chapter has led to serious problems in parts of the OECD automobile industry, and to the necessity of adopting different strategies for survival. Some main possible adjustment strategies or scenarios will be discussed here. One of these is the "world car" strategy, and the others are "specialisation" or the "technological divergence strategy". All of them involve producing cars for a "world" or "regional" rather than a national market.

It is clear that these distinctions, made for analytical reasons, hardly do justice in the present circumstances to a great variety of strategies such as joint ventures. For a number of manufacturers, the size or span of their production range rules out any pure specialisation strategy, but neither are they prepared, or in a position, to produce or assemble their products in a large number of places outside their home country. The reality of the car market is complex and could involve a number of strategies at the same time.

B. "The World Car" scenario

This refers to the concept of producing a car or a range of cars for sale in all major markets. The availability of variants of a particular type of car to suit different countries is a significant element of the world car concept whereas the fact that a particular manufacturer produces different types of car in different countries is not completely relevant to the world car concept but could also be relevant to the so-called "specialisation strategy". The difference between this and previous systems is that the cars are assembled locally to overcome tariff or non-tariff barriers on trade in finished cars. The components are produced at lower cost regional production centres and are shipped to the local assembly plants.

The form in which the trade in components takes place is of some importance. For the integrated producers making a range of products, components trade would take the form of an intra-company transfer. Fully owned component subsidiaries would be established in lower cost efficient locations which would then supply components to other subsidiaries of the same company.

A variation of this would be when the traditional domestic component supplier continues delivering components to assembly plants based in foreign countries. This would represent an extension of previous "most-favoured-customer" agreements to new locations. The advantages of such a strategy are that scale economies in component production can be reached, while dis-economies related to low assembly volumes in particular markets can be minimized.

In Table 29 a number of estimates, by various authors, for minimum efficient size by stage of manufacturing process have been given. As can be seen, the minimum efficient size of casting, machining and stamping operations tends to be higher than for final assembly. This supports the world car concept and indicates that there are advantages to having a few component manufacturing centres producing for the whole firm and supplying standardized parts for the entire model range.

A number of other advantages associated with the world car concept can also be cited. Its application would alter the pattern of international trade in automotive products away from trade in built-up cars and towards more trade in components. This might serve to reduce some of the trade frictions between trading partners, and incidentally bring about substantial changes in the component-assembler relationship.

It would also encourage the diffusion of new product and process innovations throughout the industry, and require extensive foreign direct investment by the companies in the industry. This would also go some way to spreading the benefits of growth and employment more equally through the OECD area. The world car, with its emphasis on standardization and scale economies is likely to favour the larger "integrated" producers, who already make a range of cars sharing a large number of components. It is interesting to note that it is the United States companies with their extensive foreign investments which have gone furthest towards developing this concept.

The basis for efficient production of world cars would therefore lead to the following type of industry structure: a geographical dispersion of components plants to lower cost locations. These plants would then supply their respective regions or in some cases the entire firm with particular components. Decentralized assembly is subject to the constraint that assembly volumes attain minimum efficient size. In small countries this would lead to exports of cars to neighbours as a means of attaining the necessary scale economies. But there are a number of quite considerable difficulties with the concept that suggest that it may not be taken up by all companies in the industry.

Some of the possible advantages of the world car concept have been suggested in the preceding paragraphs. There are also important drawbacks to its implementation. In Table 29 it can be seen that the minimum efficient size for assembly operations lies between 200 000 and 400 000 units. It is probable that some economies can still be gained at volumes of 500 000 units. This means that efficient production will still be limited to the larger consuming countries. Since productivity levels, especially in developing countries, are not generally equal to those obtained in the larger OECD countries, further cost increases would be incurred. The world car concept requires high technical standards and quality control in the decentralized plants. It is not always obvious that these standards can be met, especially when production is located in developing countries.

The recent application of robots to the assembly process has made the observance of certain engineering tolerances and standards more and not less important. It has also increased the need for maintenance personnel in order to ensure continuous operation. Again, skills of this kind are mostly located in the OECD area and cannot easily be transferred elsewhere. Experience of buy-back agreements from the eastern European countries had indicated that quality problems and the issue of product homologation placed limits on what could be sold on western markets in some cases. This suggests that, while the design and co-ordination of world production are not impossible, and to some extent are already applied, there are substantial difficulties that do not make the application of the world car concept straightforward.

It should also not be forgotten that world-wide production of a world car could involve a decentralization of production away from the traditional manufacturing areas. A reduction in the share of value added accounted for by the traditional producers might not be easy to obtain for political reasons. Since the industry is regionally concentrated, the reduction of output or the closure of facilities is likely to give rise to employment problems of a structural nature.

Finally the application of the world car concept could be more and more difficult to manage to respond to the more rapid changes in models, in technology, etc. In other words the flexibility of adaptation, which seems to be the characteristic of the future structure of the industry, would be more difficult to implement within this strategy. In recent years it has been the smaller size specialist producers such as Daimler Benz and BMW that have been more profitable than the mass market producers. Many of the supposed advantages of the world cars have not been realised as fully as was hoped, indeed the level of commonality and interchangeability between the North American and European version of these cars is rather low. In addition, some of the theoretical advantages of low cost production in newly industrialised countries have been offset by much lower productivity, a lower degree of system efficiency, higher component costs resulting from local content requirements and macro-economic disturbances such as rapid exchange rate changes.

C. The "Specialisation" and/or "Technological divergence" scenario

This refers to the concentration of a manufacturer on a particular segment. It entails some abandonment of trying to cover the whole market with an integrated model range. This is not done without regard for scale economies, and most of these producers do operate at the minimum efficient scale mentioned above. But scale economies are achieved less in the traditional sense of high production volumes and standardisation of components and more by the application of skill and technology to a particular type of car. This can be thought of as an increase in the division of labour and could also contribute to increased scale economies.

The "specialist" producer aims to manufacture a car which occupies some particular market niche. The product is "differentiated" from those of the volume producers so that very often an additional characteristic or service is offered. The "specialist" produces at efficient volumes for a world market and aims to sell only in that market segment. The classic examples are firms offering additional technology like: BMW – performance; Mercedes-Benz – luxury and reliability; Volvo – safety and reliability, etc.

An alternative scenario, here called the technological divergence scenario[14] and elsewhere the dematurity scenario, foresees in essence a growing spectrum of technological alternatives becoming available to meet a greater diversity of user needs and leading to a much higher priority being placed on flexibility rather than efficiency in the configuration of the production process. These developments could change the structure of the industry towards a less vertically integrated structure where medium sized producers stand a much greater chance of survival through skilful exploitation of particular technologies and market niches.

This technological scenario has some common features with the specialisation scenario. Neither envisages an almost inevitable transfer of production to lower cost locations, arguing that even mature industries can undergo a renewal through technologically driven strategies, i.e. reversing the process of maturity.

14. D. Jones (1982, b), and Abernathy, Clark, Dopico, Kantrow, Klein, Utterback.

Trade flows, within these strategies, would continue to some extent to consist of finished cars which would be exported from the traditional OECD manufacturing areas. Some foreign investment in local assembly facilities will occur, but large increases in the international trade of components would probably not be experienced. One reason for this lies in the close relationship necessary between a specialist vehicle assembler and his components supplier. A specialist vehicle requires more complex components which must be manufactured to high standards of design and reliability. The difficulty of ensuring that the component supplier also locates production abroad implies that specialist vehicle production will continue to be located in traditional areas[15].

A very theoretical variation of the market specialisation strategy could exist in that automobile producers could "specialise" in the production of components only. This would represent some sort of vertical "disintegration" of production and would also lead to an apparent increase in components trade which is hard to distinguish from an increase caused by a shift to world car type production.

In Appendix B an analysis is made of two broad indicators of direction towards the extreme scenarios, the "world car" strategy and the "specialist" strategy, namely the actual trade and market share trends, with a view to obtain some indication on their present implementation. After having analysed in that appendix recent trends in international trade in the automobile industry and the market shares of some so-called "specialist" producers, the evidence of a growth in "world" car type production does not seem very strong at least during the period covered by the analysis. Instead, the statistics suggest that, during the period, the trend towards market "specialisation" has been stronger, especially if the trend by some countries towards specialisation in components production is included. Caution however is necessary in trying to develop policy conclusions from these statistical descriptions. The automobile industry is complex and the interpenetration of various strategies, sometimes within one producer, does not allow simple conclusions to be drawn.

The following paragraphs analyse, within the main OECD producing areas, the way in which producers have reacted and could react in the future to changes in demand and supply conditions.

4. INDUSTRIES' STRATEGIC RESPONSES

The previous parts have deliberately drawn some extreme theoretical scenarios, notably those relative to the "world car" and to "specialist" and/or "technological divergence". The actual path the industry follows probably will contain some elements of these various scenarios. It is useful now to evaluate how automobile firms in the main producing regions actually pursue their strategies in relation to these scenarios.

In general, the convergent trends implied in the "world car" scenario could in the immediate future be an important factor affecting the firms' expansion or survival while the divergent trends of the alternative scenarios will only begin to have an impact as the full effects of new technologies are felt, from the second half of the 1980s onwards. In

---

15. A particular example of this can be seen in the Japanese industry. It has been argued that one of the advantages enjoyed by the Japanese industry lies in its special relationship with its suppliers. Using the 'Kan-ban' or "just-in-time" system, components are delivered virtually as they are required by the assembler. This has the advantage for the assembler of reducing storage space and inventory costs. Components are then delivered more frequently and in smaller quantities. Such a system requires the close proximity of the components suppliers to the vehicle assemblers which happens to correspond to the Japanese conditions. It is likely that the difficulties involved in transferring this system to other countries acts as a barrier to foreign investment by the Japanese automobile industry.

Similar arguments might also be applicable for the European "specialist" producers.

Europe, the pace of growth of product technology slowed down less than it did in the United States in the post-war period. European industry has been pulled in both directions, with some European firms seeking to develop a world presence and others pursing more technologically oriented strategies. Japanese firms are more oriented toward exporting complete cars than most other world producers and thus had to be more and more competitive. Their present leading role in process efficiency is widely acknowledged, while they are clearly making efforts to move production overseas.

Japan

The climb of the Japanese automobile industry to the front rank among automobile producers was the most significant structural shift in the industry in the last decade. Japanese production of automobiles rose from 4.6 to 7.0 million units between 1975 and 1980, and exports (including kits for overseas assembly) more than doubled from 1.8 to 4.2 million (around 2.0 million of these to North America and 1.0 million to Western Europe). Over the last three decades, Japanese firms have built a highly efficient production system that has clearly taken the art of mass production and scientific management a major step beyond that reached years ago in the United States and Europe. This will have major implications for the operations of producers elsewhere: the learning process – appreciating the existence of substantial differences in efficiency, digesting its full implications and implementing the lessons learnt – is now well underway in the automobile firms of North America and Western Europe, and is filtering down to the component producers also.

This efficient production system began evolving in the 1950s, with support from MITI, technology transfer and protection. The rapid growth of the automobile industry was a result of the rapid growth of the Japanese economy. Six new companies began automobile production in the early 1960s; and MITI, concerned about the competitiveness of the eleven producers, attempted to consolidate the structure of the industry. Although some mergers and takeovers took place, MITI's efforts to create two or three major producers were not realised. The resulting intensely competitive situation drove the companies relentlessly to seek ways to achieve greater efficiency. This intense intergroup competition, supplemented by the entry into the market of companies such as Honda, provided the basis for domestic competitiveness which spilled over into export competitiveness.

In the 1970s, efforts to improve efficiency shifted to integrating the chain of component producers by tying them much more into the production process through the "just-in-time" system and diffusing advanced process technology and management technologies down to these companies. The result was a highly flexible system of vertical quasi-integration which contrasts with the arm's length relationship between automobile firms and component firms in the United States and in most European countries. These close links in the Japanese automobile groups facilitate the integration of production planning, higher levels of production efficiency and product development and preserve a competitive check at each stage of the production chain.

By 1980 the Japanese industry had achieved a substantial landed cost advantage over North American and European firms. While there is general agreement on the factors that are responsible for this cost advantage, there is disagreement as to their relative importance. Most observers agree that the most significant advantage is in managerial, organisational and labour factors rather than to superior levels of automation. The dynamic advantages of integration with the component chain and the strategic back-up resulting from group membership should not be overlooked.

1980-81 will probably be recorded as a crucial period in the history of the Japanese automobile industry, as restrictions on exports to all the main automobile producing countries were introduced. Because of them, the strategies of the Japanese producers have shifted in the short run to exporting a more up-market model mix, thereby continuing to increase the value of exports in the face of volume restrictions, and increasing exports of kits for overseas assembly. In the longer term Japanese producers have begun establishing production facilities abroad, both on greenfield sites and in joint ventures with local producers. Nissan and Honda have established plants in the United States and Toyota is negotiating with General Motors to produce jointly in the United States. Nissan owns Motor Ibericain in Spain, has a joint venture with Alfa Romeo and is considering establishing a plant in the United Kingdom; Honda and British Leyland, and Nissan and Volkswagen, have licence production agreements. The great challenge facing Japanese companies in going offshore is how to successfully transfer their own management practices to a non-Japanese environment. Further moves in this direction can be expected in the 1980s, as the momentum for further offshore investment grows and more internationally-oriented management takes over in Japan.

Japanese production now is heavily concentrated in the light- to medium-sized sectors of the market, with a major emphasis on the production of more economic cars to help maintain demand. Two major producers are planning to introduce very small cars, first on the domestic market. For the above reasons some shift towards producing more medium- and large-sized cars would also be expected. The pattern of demand in the Japanese domestic market is a constraint on such a move towards producing large sized cars. This problem is not experienced by German and US producers.

More important for the future, Japanese producers have been investing heavily in recent years in new technology, innovation and research and development. Already by 1977, Japanese producers employed 34 000 in R&D (compared with 23 000 in FR Germany) and were spending 8 per cent more than their German counterparts. Since then, the differences have almost certainly widened. Another hint of this investment in technology is seen in patenting behaviour. Patenting can be seen as both a portfolio of

Table 33.   **Automobile patents registered in the United States**

	Number				Percentage			
	1965/6	1970/1	1975/6	1980/1	1965/6	1970/1	1975/6	1980/1
Motor Vehicles[2]								
United States	1 700	1 637	1 854	2 661	—	—	—	—
United States (16 %)[1]	272	262	297	426	32.9	26.7	19.2	25.0
Japan	28	98	328	513	3.4	10.0	21.2	30.1
F.R. Germany	201	251	385	356	24.3	25.5	24.9	20.9
United Kingdom	120	128	163	103	14.5	13.0	10.6	6.1
France	85	84	138	88	10.3	8.5	8.9	5.2
Foreign	556	721	1 238	1 276	—	—	—	—
Subtotal[1]	828	983	1 545	1 702	100.0	100.0	100.0	100.0
Engines and Turbines[2]								
United States	1 309	1 060	1 368	1 963	—	—	—	—
United States (16 %)[1]	209	170	219	314	29.1	18.6	20.6	25.5
Japan	36	64	230	373	5.0	7.0	21.7	30.3
F.R. Germany	162	221	244	224	22.6	24.2	23.0	18.2
United Kingdom	126	119	105	87	17.6	13.0	9.9	7.1
France	61	52	96	66	8.5	5.7	9.0	5.4
Foreign	508	744	842	915	—	—	—	—
Subtotal[1]	717	914	1 061	1 229	100.0	100.0	100.0	100.0

1.   The proportion of domestically registered patents in the United States that are also registered abroad averages 16 % in both Western Europe and Japan. For closer comparability foreign patents registered in the United States have been equated with this reduced number of US patents in estimating shares.
2.   Motor vehicles (US SIC 371). Internal combustion engines account for an overwhelming proportion of patents in engines and turbines (US SIC 351).
Source :   Data estimated by D. Jones, SPRU, from data supplied by OTAF, Washington.

technological options open to the firm and an indication of the thoroughness of the process of incremental improvement. As an example, Table 33 shows relative patenting behaviour in motor vehicles and engines in the United States. Given the possible shift in competitiveness in automobiles to emphasize technical progress such as fuel economy, the Japanese automobile industry looks well placed to compete on this front in the future.

To summarise, the Japanese firms' strategy has given them a world lead in process efficiency, and probably also placed them in a good position in product technology in the future. Combined with a shift towards installing plants offshore, this strategy will clearly give Japanese manufacturers a leading role in this industry for some time to come. Some uncertainty remains about the ability to translate Japanese management practices overseas and the ability to manage the structural adjustment domestically as productivity improves and the industry moves offshore.

United States

In the face of growing imports of small cars after the first oil shock of 1973, US producers initiated a massive programme to downsize their entire model range and practically rebuild their production facilities by 1985. The scale of the programme was then put at $80 billion. US producers saw that they were losing market shares as they were unable to meet demand for smaller models, because of their inadequate production expertise or facilities for smaller cars. US car-makers felt that after a period of readjustment and the establishment of a new dominant design for the rest of the 1980s, the industry would be able to regain market shares and roll back imports.

Thus US producers began to exploit their network of production facilities around the world, to gain economies of scale through common designs producible in multiple locations and to source standardized components from the most advantageous locations and tranship them from one location to another. General Motors envisaged standardizing their fleet around a few models worldwide. Ford were slower off the mark in downsizing; their first "world car", the Escort, only appeared in 1981. This cost them market share in the United States. However Ford already had some experience in integrating production facilities and standardizing models in Europe. In Europe General Motors was slower to integrate its subsidiaries in FR Germany and in the United Kingdom. Chrysler, without the resources of the big two, was forced to abandon certain market segments, and, later, to sell off its European operations to Peugeot and import cars from Mitsubishi and engines from Volkswagen, Peugeot and Mitsubishi to fill its model range.

In the middle of this downsizing programme, the US market went into steep decline from 9.3 million US-built sales in 1978 to 6.2 million in 1981. At the same time, imports from Japan continued to rise, even after the introduction of downsized models from all three main producers. The situation became critical at Chrysler and in 1979 the government was forced to come to the rescue with a series of credit guarantees. Between 1973 and 1978, furthermore, the pattern of demand reverted, to some extent, to larger cars. After the 1979 oil shock, it seems to have changed direction again.

As the situation got steadily worse and new downsized models failed to stem the import tide, it became clear that the problems of the US industry were structural. In 1978 about 2 million people were employed by the assemblers and suppliers; at least 500 000 of these employees have been laid off or made redundant over the last two years. Plants were closed and others mothballed. The comparatively high wages in the car industry is one element which resulted in lower productivity than in Japan (and probably to a smaller extent than in Europe). The responsibility for this divergence between productivity and remuneration lies both with management and labour, and the two parties needed to begin to move towards reducing the cost disparity. This was achieved by allowing Union of Automobile Workers to sit on the board of some corporations, and, in 1980 and 1981, by renegotiating wage agreements with all the producers. This process will have to continue over many years, accompanied by efforts to increase productivity.

Changes in management attitudes and practices have begun to revolutionise the way in which production has been organised. They are also beginning to change the traditionally very loose relationships with component suppliers. Companies are also changing their attitudes towards a more co-operative relationship and towards the development of new production equipment. Whereas US producers, unlike Japanese or European firms, normally left the development of machinery to specialist firms, they have now embarked on a very ambitious programme of developing robots and automated production systems in-house.

Heavy capital expenditure in response to the Japanese cost advantage, together with the need for an expensive second generation of downsized models, is putting additional strain on the already stretched financial position of all three producers. Moreover the US financial system, which tends to focus on short-term performance, does not reward the companies' attempts to develop new longer term strategies to meet these structural problems. Companies in Japan and FR Germany, with closer long-term involvement with their financial institutions, and those in France, with a similar relationship with the government which now has control of all the nationalised banks, are not faced with these kinds of constraints on their behaviour.

At the international level, little is heard of the world car. US producers are looking more and more to sourcing at least the smaller end of their model range together with engines and components from outside the United States. General Motors plans to source one model in Japan, produced by Isuzu in which GM has a major holding, and is negotiating for joint production of a mid-sized model in the United States with Toyota, with probably some content originating in Japan. Ford's links with Toyo Kogyo, and Chrysler's with Mitsubishi and Peugeot may evolve in a similar direction. Engine outsourcing is already well advanced and some specialists estimate that up to 3.3 million engines will come from Mexico, Brazil, Canada, Japan and France in model year 1983. In addition, the import of other components is expected to grow. The extent of the shift to outsourcing will partly depend on labour agreements in future years and on political developments in relation to protectionism.

Political pressures for some form of protection grew as the crisis of the US industry deepened and in response the Japanese agreed to voluntarily restrain exports. Japanese exports to the United States fell from 1.8 million in 1980 to 1.76 million in 1981 and to 1.68 million in 1982. While this gave the US industry a breathing space it also incited the Japanese to move upmarket in their product mix. Recent suggestions to tighten the restrictions by introducing local content rules highlighted the dilemma facing the US companies: any tighter restrictions on imports would jeopardise plans to outsource models, engines and components. The uncertainty about this political dimension makes forward strategic planning more difficult for the US producers.

In summary, the US producers have many structural problems to solve and the future shape of the industry in the United States will change as a result, as some Japanese producers join Volkswagen and Renault (which has taken control of American Motors) as US producers. The main problems of US firms are not in product technology; both Ford and GM have access to successful models in their European operations. The problems are more to do with realising that market forces have changed fundamentally, and with developing and implementing strategies accordingly. Although much has changed in recent years, there is still scope for improving the nature and orientation of US companies' relations with labour, government and finance in order to support international competitiveness.

The two distinguishing characteristics of the Western European situation compared with Japan or the United States are the much greater diversity of markets and the greater number of producers of both mass market and specialist cars.

Including the European divisions of Ford and General Motors, six major producers in Europe will be turning out over 1 million cars a year by 1983. Of the other full range producers, British Leyland is struggling to recover lost ground and Seat is renegotiating licence agreements with other producers. Europe's strength in producing small cars is evident: Fiat, Renault and Peugeot-Citroën each produce more of what might be called micro-minis than the whole of the Japanese industry combined.

European producers collectively still have an advantage in automotive technology, particularly product technology (see Table 33). The importance attached to maintaining this European strength is underlined by official support for new technology in this industry in Germany, France and Italy.

Staying ahead in automotive technology obviously has been the central element in the strategies of some specialised producers such as Daimler Benz and BMW, and it is now perceived as crucial by all the other major producers. The only other company whose survival has hinged on product technology is Saab, whose early introduction of the turbocharger is acknowledged to have saved the firm in recent years. In future, the emphasis in France will be heavily oriented towards further reducing costs and improving general efficiency, through incorporating new materials and manufacturing techniques and more fuel-efficient engines. This emphasis is being reinforced by the priorities of government technology policies in relation to the automobile of the future. Fiat is following a similar path, through the introduction of advanced manufacturing technologies and possibly a large degree of bodywork plastics. Volvo and Alfa Romeo have sought to exploit niches in the market, the former successfully in large family transports and the latter less so for more sporting cars.

In addition to moving upmarket in response to import competition, there are a number of other ways in which European firms have improved their efficiency in recent years. Volkswagen, Renault and Fiat, notably, are doing so on the basis of product technology developed in-house. Volkswagen and Renault have not been willing to sell this technology to other companies. Fiat has done so, initially to Eastern European countries; this was the result of a deliberate diversification strategy in the early 1970s, when for a time the development of non-automotive activities was given high priority.

Joint ventures may offer economies of scale in design and production in Europe. European producers have entered into a variety of such relationships: for instance the long-standing joint production of engines between Renault and Peugeot, and in one case with Volvo; joint gearbox development between Renault and Volkswagen; and joint engine production between Peugeot and Fiat. Cross-supply of key components from one producer to the other is also developing, for instance gearboxes from VW to British Leyland and diesel engines from Peugeot to Ford. Smaller companies have also sought co-operation with larger producers, notably the Volvo-Renault, Saab-Fiat Lancia, Alfa Romeo-Nissan and British Leyland-Honda links.

In addition to horizontal co-operation between automobile producers, considerable changes are taking place in the relations with component suppliers in Europe. Major changes in management practices and new automated production equipment are being diffused to components suppliers as part of the cost-cutting strategies of the automobile firms. This has also been accompanied by mergers and rationalisation in the structure of the components industry. Although some cross-border mergers have been frustrated in the past by anti-trust regulations, further rationalisation of the components industry in Europe should certainly continue. At the same time, the components industry is being called upon more and more to share the burden of innovation and product design. Whether this will lead to a more vertically structured relationship in Europe similar to that in Japan, or to the survival of a number of strong independent component producers supplying producers throughout Europe, is an open question.

Another strategy in the face of Japanese competition has been to seek some measure of protection from Japanese imports. A tight quota on Japanese cars has existed in Italy since before its entry into the EC. In France, Japanese car imports have been restricted to 3 per cent of the market since 1977. The UK producers have had discussions since 1975 with Japanese producers on a number of issues, and sales of Japanese cars have been about 11 per cent of the UK market. In 1981, following Japanese export restraint on the US market and to avoid possible trade diversions, imports to Benelux and FR Germany were also downgraded without any explicit governmental or producers arrangements.

In addition to seeking higher productivity at home, some of the European producers have sought to join General Motors and Ford in the league of multinational producers. Volkswagen and Renault have been the most active in this regard. Volkswagen began production in the United States in 1978 and has developed the largest presence in Latin America. Nissan will be producing a Volkswagen car in Japan for sale in Japan, where Volkswagen is the largest importer, and in South East Asia. Production of smaller VW cars in Spain at Seat is under negotiation. Renault has begun to produce a car in the United States, having taken a controlling share in American Motors, though its biggest foreign production bases are in Spain and Portugal. Peugeot now produces cars only in Europe, having pulled out of its joint venture with Fiat in Argentina, though it maintains links with Chrysler. After leaving Seat in Spain, the share of Fiat's foreign production has diminished; like other producers in Latin America, it has experienced substantial losses in Brazil and Argentina. However, its licence production agreements with Poland and Yugoslavia give it a particularly large presence in Eastern Europe.

EVOLUTION OF THE CONCEPT OF EXCESS CAPACITY

It is interesting to examine in parallel the prospect for demand for cars as analysed in Chapter II, and that for supply, with a view to discerning the emergence in the longer term of excess capacity.

This Chapter highlighted what seems to have become a major characteristic of the industry: an increasing flexibility of response to technical and structural trends. It is useful, in this context, to reflect on the concept of surplus capacity both now and in the longer term.

Table 1 of Chapter I showed output figures, including production achieved in peak periods which could be considered as the practical capacity. If these figures are examined (bearing in mind what has been said on trends in technology, localisation and structures), their mathematical, and thus fragmentary, nature becomes evident. One important element, the qualitative element of car production capacity is not taken into account.

Historical production data provide weak and not objective grounds for assumptions about excess capacity. In an industry in permanent and rapid evolution, capacity can be calculated only in relation to a precisely-defined production programme. Switches in demand from some models or some series of models and fittings to others can lead to substantial discrepancies between technologically and commercially usable capacity. It is also necessary to take into account the quantity and the quality of the available labour force. Changes in working hours or the number of shifts worked may have considerable implications for output. Car engineering and production technology may also affect quantitative capacity.

The example of the United States is worth noting. In 1980, the United States imported some 2.8 million foreign cars in response to a domestic demand for smaller and more fuel-efficient cars. There was thus in that country, and in that period, an evident excess capacity for larger cars. Some Ford and General Motors plants have been closed – in many cases definitively – with all the painful labour problems involved in such adaptation.

This suggests that excess capacity in the coming years will be increasingly linked to the launching of new models and to the introduction of new product and process technologies. The increased flexibility that the industry will have acquired could ease the transitional periods but it is evident that, locally and during some periods, excess capacity will temporarily exist. Governments should ensure that, by appropriate multilateral information and discussion, trade problems which could arise are dealt with without provoking protectionist chain reactions.

5. GOVERNMENTS AND THE STRUCTURAL ADJUSTMENT OF THE AUTOMOBILE INDUSTRY

In view of the motor industry crisis during the late 1970s and early 1980s, government intervention could become increasingly common. By and large, governments have not so far intervened in manufacturers' international strategy decisions; in most producer countries, action by central government has tended to be national, large scale and not always consistent. With the growing internationalisation of the motor industry which this report has attempted to highlight, the national approach is becoming outdated. This is already apparent at the level of the European Community and it is likely to become even more clear at the international level for the major producer countries, and at world level. In the next chapter an attempt is made to suggest possible responses to this situation.

Since the purpose of this report is to outline likely future trends and problems in the motor industry, the intention in the present section is not to compile an inventory of past and present government action, but merely to highlight its main features, its overall philosophy and its aspects which will have an impact on the four main avenues of government action. These latter include competition policy, specific or technical measures of assistance, measures to facilitate structural adjustment and measures to facilitate technological innovations. Some paragraphs of this chapter deal with trade. The implications for the future to be drawn from this analysis are dealt with more specifically in the next chapter.

Competition Policies

Policies which governments may introduce, for whatever reason, to regulate competition and industrial concentration, play a major role in the way the motor industry adapts to the increasing internationalisation of production and products.

Current policies in the three producer regions – the United States, the EEC and Japan – are briefly analysed in the following paragraphs.

In the United States anti-trust laws reflect the basic attitude of successive administrations towards the economy and industry: free competition guarantees economic efficiency and consumer welfare. Thus, the job of government is not to impose a structural policy but only to ensure that free competition is preserved.

Over the past 50 years, the automobile industry in the United States has been an object of virtually constant scrutiny from this standpoint. This did not prevent the development of very large firms – even if, on occasion, rulings were made against mergers in which parts manufacturers would have been taken over. Perhaps this is due to a certain fundamental contradiction: although the philosophy underlying US anti-trust legislation is the defence of free enterprise, its application can easily take on the appearance of a policy concerned with the structure of industry, which is exactly what governments wished to avoid. This may explain the sometimes highly legalistic character of the US system as well as its somewhat pragmatic aspects (such as the "rule of reason" which requires that an analysis of market conditions, among other things, is taken into consideration). In their decisions the courts generally confine their reference to the domestic market and to such factors as market shares, number of firms, etc. Dynamic market forces, such as technological competition and the internationalisation of markets are rarely brought up.

In the European Community, anti-trust and competition policies are decided at both national and Community level (in accordance with Articles 85 and 86 of the Treaty of Rome). In most national legislation, a "dominant position" as such is not unlawful, only its misuse. The Commission of the European Communities "has the power to forbid an abusive reinforcement, by concentration, of a dominant position held by one or more undertakings".

The Commission has recently pointed out[16] that "comparison of the market shares of the four largest European manufacturers of cars and commercial vehicles and of the European subsidiaries of two North American groups permits the conclusion that no manufacturer has as yet achieved such a dominant position within the Common Market."

The maintenance of a balanced, competitive oligopoly implies the necessity of preventing abusive reinforcements of dominant positions, which would remove from the market the balancing force which is indispensable to the free play of effective competition; it is, however, impossible to lay down in advance and in the abstract the size which a single undertaking should not exceed, or what constitutes a sufficient number of competitors.

The Commission exercises the power of forbidding agreements which limit competition in the Common Market and authorising co-operation which brings advantages both for the productivity of undertakings and for consumers. For example, co-operation agreements concerning research, development and larger-scale production of components necessary for vehicle manufacture have always been accepted by the Commission, in view in particular of the rationalisation benefits which result.

The anti-trust laws in Japan date from 1947 and are similar in principle to those of the United States: they outlaw all forms of cartel which substantially reduce competition and which are contrary to public interest. However, although the legislation itself, which is administered by an independent "Fair Trade Commission", may seem fairly strict, a series of exemptions has been gradually introduced, e.g. as in the case of "depression" or "rationalisation" cartels in a period of economic recession. One of these exemptions in the field of automobile concerns the rationalisation of the tyre industry.

It might be noted at this point that, in measures affecting the car industry's structure, both the Europeans and the Japanese seem to pay more attention than the Americans to the outlook for the world market as a whole, the need to be competitive internationally and the industry's increasing international character. In the United States, it was not until very recently that any serious thinking was applied to the problem.

16. *The European automobile industry*, Commission statement (1981).

Trends in government intervention

The following paragraphs do not deal with general policies in areas such as road-building, decentralisation, etc., which may encourage or discourage the growth of the motor industry. The measures discussed here can be classified as those:

   i)   which are not directly related to problems of industrial adjustment or restructuring, such as measures of a more technical nature concerned with environmental protection, safety and economy;

  ii)   prompted by the crisis in the industry and designed to save or improve existing industrial structures;

 iii)   intended to develop the potential for technological adjustment; and

 iv)   issues in the trade area.

Measures of a specific or technical nature

By and large, government policies in fields not directly connected with the structure of the industry have been designed to minimise the adverse effects of the increasing use of motor vehicles. Cases in point are measures on safety, air pollution and noise, energy consumption, etc. The purpose of these specific and generally somewhat technical regulations is to reduce the public or social cost of the use of the car, but they also have an impact on the scale of car use and the types of vehicle used. They may, of course, as already indicated, also have an effect on industry or international trade, generally unintended. One area for increased international co-operation in the future might be the assurance that such national regulations do not lead to major distortions in international trade. Work done in international organisations on this subject should be more effectively supported by all governments.

Measures to facilitate structural adjustment

The worldwide economic recession in the wake of the series of oil shocks since 1974 has sharply highlighted the structural shortcomings of the motor industry in many manufacturing countries. Several governments, in theory adverse to any kind of interventionism, have been obliged to act in an attempt to limit the industrial and, above all, social consequences of unduly rapid structural adjustment.

In the United States the debate as to what policy should be adopted as regards the automobile industry is still going on but some tendencies seem to be emerging. Having obtained some respite from Japanese car imports so that the process of adjusting the industry's structures might be less abrupt, the government decided to relax the regulatory constraints, particularly as regards the environment and fuel cosumption. These had been a heavy drain on the industry's investment capability. At the same time, the government guaranteed a substantial loan to save Chrysler from bankruptcy and enable the company to work on a plan to recover its competitiveness. So, although the government is not intervening directly in the strategy of the firm, it is doing what it can to create the conditions for what is regarded as an essential restructuring operation.

In Europe government intervention may take different forms for historical reasons and also because of differing economic philosophies. In the Federal Republic of Germany, there has been no government intervention in the structural changes in the industry, reflecting the prevalent economic philosophy. In France, preserving the existing structure of the motor industry, which consists of one state-owned group, and one privately-owned group is a constant Governmental concern. Although the State normally does not intervene in the management or industrial strategy of either, it has been at pains to ensure the balanced development of both these key firms. In the United Kingdom a series of mergers and amalgamations have taken place since 1954, sometimes with government help, in a bid to improve the competitive position of motor industry groups by economies of scale. These moves, however, failed to withstand the shocks suffered by the economy since 1973. The largest group was nationalised in 1975 and, until recently, it was still having difficulty finding the necessary funds for its investment programme.

In most other European countries (Italy, Sweden, Spain, etc.) the overall pattern is similar to that in these three major manufacturing countries. Although, in principle, government does not interfere in the management and strategy of the motor firms, whether nationalised or not, in practice it has been unable to ignore the difficulties of an industry providing so many jobs and therefore politically sensitive.

Basically, the situation in Japan is fairly similar, despite significant minor differences as a result of the country's different historical and cultural development. Industrial strategies are decided by industry: the role of the government and, in particular, of the MITI is to provide a suitably favourable environment. This was very clear during the development stage of the Japanese automobile industry in the 1950s and even the 1960s.

It is true that in most major manufacturing countries the government refrains from interfering directly in the long-term structural development of the motor industry. Yet government influence has increased markedly in most countries in recent years, particularly in terms of the aid it provides to ailing firms, the expansion of the public sector in certain countries and the support and overall policy guidance it provides. In addition, many countries have introduced short-term, trade-related measures designed to help domestic industries through the difficult but vital phase of reorganisation. These will be discussed later.

Measures to facilitate technological innovation

The intention in the following paragraphs is not to list the various measures that governments have adopted to promote technological progress, but rather to summarise the thinking which appears to be behind them and which could be applied in the future.

Historically, the major portion of the US industry's technological effort was directed at developing both products with enhanced consumer appeal and more efficient manufacturing processes. Basic research was not emphasized. In the 1960s, the US initiated a government-financed applied research programme for advanced automotive power systems. This ongoing research is carried out by Government laboratories and a number of companies both within and outside the automobile industry. In 1979, the Government proposed a joint government-industry basic research programme aimed at substantially improving motor vehicle fuel efficiency. This programme, which was intended to complement the alternative engine effort, was never started.

In Europe, product-oriented technological R&D has always been considered a key to success in the market. Major motor manufacturers elsewhere have often relied on technology of European origin for their development. The governments in most of the major European producer countries participate in one way or another in both product and process R&D. According to the Commission of the European Communities, however, car manufacturers have "lost some of their lead over foreign – and in particular Japanese – industries, where extensive research and development work has been carried out"[17]. The Commission adds that "because of the increasing importance of the economies of scale which can be achieved financially and industrially, the only solution once again seems to be co-operation and co-ordination". A significant example is the

17. *The European Automobile Industry*, Commission Statement (1981).

co-operation between Renault, PSA, BL, Fiat, VW and Volvo in a Joint Research Committee.

Technological development was not the prime aim of the automobile industry in Japan during its period of rapid growth. In recent years, however, activity in this area has become crucially important as a means of ensuring that Japanese products retain their competitiveness vis-à-vis foreign makers and maintaining Japan's competitive edge in production costs. Direct government intervention in research is relatively rare. Policy tends to lean toward indirect encouragement, as in the case of government promotion of robot development, the principal user of which is the automobile industry.

Issues in the trade area

It is necessary, at the end of this part, to deal briefly with the trade area. As this report has shown, the automobile market has become an international one; and the structure of industries has adapted, and will continue to adapt, to this trend. Fundamentally, the automobile industries can operate with full efficiency only in the context of international free trade. Global tariff negotiations have facilitated this trend.

However, in the last few years – and as the world economy has slowed down – policies or practices have developed in many countries which tend to restrict trade flows. This phenomenon appeared first in countries where, for political reasons, governments imposed import restrictions to help develop a national automobile industry. Then the very rapid development of Japanese exports triggered a protectionist reflex in industrialised countries which already had an automobile industry. In economies already affected by high unemployment, the object was – and still is – to keep alive a labour-intensive, strategic industry and to not exacerbate internal tension.

Regulatory, voluntary or de facto restrictions on exports or imports have developed in many Member and non-Member countries. The concept of "local content", which requires that a manufacturer producing in another country employ some percentage of local labour force, components, etc. from the host country, has spread in developing and developed countries alike. The Japanese automobile industry estimates, for instance, that at least 40 per cent of the world market in 1982 is affected by various restrictions on Japanese exports. Industries in other countries are also affected, probably in smaller proportions.

These practices evidently run counter to the free trade principles continually advocated by the automobile industry. In the current world economic context, the collapse or the sudden contraction of a national automobile industry would be unacceptable for most governments. If the automobile industry wants, in the longer term, to return to a healthy situation where free-trade would be the rule and not the exception, and where government intervention would be limited to the minimum, all producers should, especially during difficult periods, voluntarily and on the basis of their knowledge, understanding and mutual acceptance of their problems, reinforce their responsiveness to developments and design their strategies taking all factors into account. Governments also have a role to play in this context; this point will be discussed further in the conclusions.

Annex

THE IMPACT OF INDUSTRIAL ROBOTS
ON THE AUTOMOBILE INDUSTRY

Introduction

The evolution of automobile production methods over the years has been towards standardization and the reliance on the efficiency of mass-production methods. The trend in automation of production in the pre-war years, as well as significant improvements in the 1950s and early 1960s, enabling mass production techniques to be applied to automobile production, led to the maintenance of relatively low product prices and to a product which became widely available as a mass consumer good.

Automation which affected the industry took place particularly in the engine plant, in the manufacture of body parts, whereas in final vehicle assembly the impact of automation has been much less. Some aspects of these changes should be noted. Firstly, they led to a high growth in productivity. Secondly, there was considerable labour shedding particularly during the early 1960s in areas such as engine assembly. Thirdly, standardization and mass production led to the use of highly dedicated capital goods.

The latter meant that production became relatively inflexible. For example, small design changes required heavy investment for retooling and often plant shutdown for several months. Thus, there was a tendency to minimise such changes, particularly in highly automated facilities such as an engine plant. As a consequence, it could be argued[1] that, despite the high volume throughput and higher productivity of dedicated facilities, in the longer run technical innovation was retarded. As a consequence, productivity growth also declined.

The decline in productivity growth, combined with an increasing cost-squeeze as a result of high and growing hourly labour costs, shifted producer emphasis towards increasing plant efficiency. Thus, in the late 1960s, a slow trend began towards the introduction of more automated production methods in the automobile assembly plant itself which, nevertheless, remained the most labour-intensive area. For example, in 1969 the first industrial robots were introduced in welding and painting in the assembly line. However, partly because of technological constraints and partly because vehicle sales remained buoyant, the emphasis by many producers on productivity improvements remained fairly marginal. Recent exogeneous shocks on the industry, particularly fuel price increases, the slowdown in demand growth and the erosion of market shares as a result of intensified international competition, have placed pressure on automobile producers to move away from dedicated machinery, suitable only for non-variable mass produced products, towards flexible production methods.

The reduced reliance by automobile producers on specialised machinery in favour of more flexible automation, which is offered by industrial robots and other CAD/CAM equipment, is viewed as necessary because:

i) there is need to reduce costs and increase productivity in the face of international competition;
ii) anticipated rapid technological change, both product and process, can be integrated more easily;
iii) the uncertainty in demand, both in volume, as well as product type, can be handled more easily.

On the cost side, rising labour costs combined with declining labour productivity have been usually cited by producers as the main factor in reducing their ability to compete effectively. Factors such as increased product quality and reliability are also playing a major role in the strategy of producers to improve competitivity.

On the technological side, the existing product offered by automobile producers and market requirements are not in equilibrium given consumer emphasis on energy-saving, safety and reliability. This implies that extensive product innovation over the next decade is required, and may also be necessary, in order to expand

---

1. See, for example, Abernathy, W. J., *The Productivity Dilemma: Roadblock to Innovation in the Automobile Industry*, Johns Hopkins University Press, Baltimore 1978.

96

markets by increasing replacement rates by offering a new, more innovative product. If this does not occur, the approach to automobile demand saturation in many countries would indicate even lower growth rates in the future as compared to the present rates[2].

Impact on Automobile Production Structure and Costs

The prospect of declining rates of growth in demand vis-à-vis existing production capacity levels would indicate that in the long term the automobile industry may face a period of mergers and capacity rationalisation. This could arise since it would become more difficult for some producers to maintain an economic level of output as more efficient producers increase their market share. A tendency toward rationalisation will be reinforced by flexible automation techniques which will enable production capacity to meet changing demand levels, changing model styles and technological requirements fairly easily.

Standardization and efficiency through economies of scale have become the norm in the automobile industry. As a corollary the production process became more rigid as the level of mechanisation increased and production became dependent on specialised equipment. The importance of the present developments in flexible automation is that such equipment allows producers to move away from rigid mass production methods allowing product changes to be incorporated without the need to scrap expensive dedicated machinery[3].

Two aspects of the increased flexibility in production need noting. Firstly, the concept of minimum efficient scale for an automobile assembly plant as well as for such components as an engine or transmission plant is changing. For example, a plant producing 400 000 vehicles a year was considered as an optimum size whereas, with increased automation, manufacturers are considering a plant with a throughput of about 250 000 vehicles as optimum. The reduced minimum efficient scale could, based on the expectation of continued slow growth in demand in the medium term, allow many of the larger firms to rationalise capacity by adopting flexible automation without altering unit costs and profits[4]. Under a production structure where 400 000 units a year was optimum, smaller firms operating at this scale would suffer if, as a result of eroding market shares, they had to adjust capacity. Rationalisation based on flexible automation would also allow such firms to adjust successfully[5].

The second aspect of increased flexibility in production relates to the ability to incorporate product changes easily. This will allow technological changes to be adopted more easily than in the past since the production equipment used is less dedicated. In the longer term, therefore, production flexibility will help stimulate technological change and facilitate innovation. In addition, exogenous shocks such as fuel price increases, environmental concerns, etc., which have provided an impetus for technical change in automobiles can be incorporated much easier and at a lower cost. The net result of increased production flexibility in the long run could be a reduction in investment requirements in the industry by eliminating the need for constant retooling to meet product and component changes. This reduction in investment requirement could, besides cost savings, have an impact on the traditional linkages between the automobile producers and the machine tool industry.

However, in the short to medium term, investment requirements for automobile producers will be high as they rationalise and modernise existing plants. Many of the projected investment requirements of major producers remain high up to the end of the 1980s. The requirement for high levels of investment at a time when profits are being squeezed by a slowdown in demand could cause problems for some companies, particularly the smaller companies and those with cash problems, and may also retard investment in flexibile automation.

Flexibility in assembling different models and the subsequent savings from avoiding frequent retooling is an important factor in stimulating the application of industrial robots in automobile production and in reducing, in the long term, the growth of unit costs. However, additional important motives exist primarily aimed at reducing costs. These include:

i) The reliability and accuracy of industrial robots ensures better quality control and consistency in product quality, reducing warranty claims, the need for a large number of quality inspectors (about 10 per cent of an assembly plant labour force), and the rate of rejections, as well as resulting in material saving.

2. See, for example, *Long Term Perspectives of the World Automobile Industry*, Chapter II, OECD 1983.
3. A recent example is an attempt by the Ford Motor Company to lower unit costs through large-scale production in a new engine-block factory which turned out to be too inflexible to be efficient. The inability to convert the casting plant to build smaller engines efficiently led to its closure.
4. A recent report by an investment analyst in the United States has indicated that break-even points by the major producers have been significantly reduced: GM from 6 million to 4.8 million units, Ford from 4.2 million to 3 million units and Chrysler from 2.2 million to 1.3 million units. This change in break-even levels is indicative of the extent to which producers are reducing their overhead costs in conjunction with efforts to increase manufacturing efficiency.
5. While minimum efficient scale for a plant may change, economies of scale for automobile production as a whole will remain important, particularly as regards standardized components, which are used in a large variety of models (e.g. engines, transmissions), and the need to compete on a world-class manufacturer. In addition, a wide model range assembled in one plant will allow for lower unit costs – such wide ranges are usually available only from the larger producers.

ii) Industrial robots provide the flexibility to cope with temporary peaks in production requirements for various models without the necessity of maintaining idle capacity or large inventories to meet these peaks. Considerable savings through the reduction of inventory requirements are also facilitated through new computerised inventory control systems, robotised warehousing, etc.

iii) computer-aided manufacturing systems increase management control and the ability to reduce bottlenecks;

iv) CAM systems and industrial robots reduce handling time per vehicle by increasing throughput and reducing direct labour costs per vehicle;

v) the reduction in labour costs.

The immediate impact in the introduction of flexible automation will thus be a reduction in, or at least the maintenance of, the real price of new motor vehicles. This is an important consideration, not only in the face of intensified international competition, but also given the need to stimulate new car and replacement demand during the present low growth period.

The present emphasis in the automobile industry on increasing productivity and therefore adopting flexibile automation could have signficant employment repercussions in an industry which in many Member countries is a major employer[6]. The impact on labour arises mainly from the intensified international competition which has led to the need to increase productivity. Since labour costs account for about 35 per cent of the total cost of a vehicle, particular emphasis is placed and will be placed on increasing labour productivity and thus reducing labour costs.

The demand situation affecting the automobile industry has led many producers, over the last few years, to reduce their labour force through rationalisation, elimination of second shifts, attrition, etc. It could therefore be argued that the increasing use of flexible automation may result in the maintenance of existing employment levels without significant further reductions in the event of a demand recovery. However, such a scenario is unlikely, given the major emphasis by producers in reducing costs, in rationalising facilities and in modernising plant and equipment. This emphasis is in particular being placed on the increased use of industrial robots in areas where robotisation techniques are now becoming fairly standard (e.g. spot-welding, painting, handling) and ultimately at assembly areas where in the past cost reductions have been difficult to implement. In all these cases, robots are usually used as a direct replacement for labour.

Applications of Robots and their Impact

To assess the impact of industrial robots on the automobile industry, specific examples of productivity or labour impact have to be examined. These examples, either individual company cases or more general situations, are often of general validity given the fairly homogeneous production structure in the industry.

Automobile production, because of the variety of operations, is highly suited for the wide application of different types of industrial robots and other forms of automated manufacturing equipment. The production process for automobiles involves:

i) casting (to produce cylinder blocks, cylinders, transmission cases, etc.);

ii) forging (gears, shafts, etc.);

iii) sintering (engine and transmission parts);

iv) heat treating (usually for hardening parts required to withstand friction);

v) machine processing and attaching (i.e. machining parts and assembly of parts);

vi) plastic forming;

vii) metal stamping;

viii) welding;

ix) painting;

x) assembly, and

xi) inspection.

Many of these processes are already areas where industrial robots have been introduced successfully in the metallurgical industries or within the automobile industry. In addition, frequent design and stylistic changes, as well as changes in parts and components, have encouraged the use of computer-aided design systems and the interface between CAD systems and machining centres[7]. The large number of parts involved in assembly are stimulating use of computer-aided manufacturing systems particularly for inventory control and management.

As the world's largest automobile producer, the production and technology strategy followed by General Motors will have important implications, not only on the robot producing industry, but also for other

6. For example, it has been estimated that 1 out of every 5 workers in the United States is either directly or indirectly employed in the motor vehicle industries. In France, 15 per cent of manufacturing employment depends on the motor vehicle industry, and in Germany about 14 per cent.

7. In the United States, the use of CAD systems in the automobile industry is growing at an annual rate of 40 per cent. CAD systems are being used extensively, for example, at Ford Motor Company to undertake all electrical design work, 50 per cent of new body components and 25 per cent of other components. At Chrysler, CAD is used to design 85 per cent of passenger vehicle bodies, 60 per cent of suspension systems and 40 per cent of engine components. [*Source:* American Metal Market News, 19th April, 1982.]

automobile producing companies. GM is presently using about 450 robots and is expected by the end of 1982 to be using, or have on order 1 600 robots. By 1985 the company plans to use about 5 000 robots worldwide, increasing to 14 000 by 1990. Of these about 5 000 will be for assembly use, 4 000 for machine loading and 1 000 will be painting robots. GM's requirements are likely to be upgraded on the basis of further technological advances in industrial robots particularly for assembly use.

The investment cost for GM's programme is expected to be significant since it would include the direct cost of industrial robots (about US$1 billion) plus ancillary equipment as well as plant modifications. Based on a criterion used by GM and other producers that a robot must replace at least two workers to be cost effective, the employment impact would be at minimum a reduction of 28 000 workposts worldwide. The usage and therefore impact of robots will vary from company to company depending on the degree of vertical integration within the company, as well as on other factors. For example, GM has internal stamping, casting and machining plants whereas other companies rely on outside contractors. In contrast to GM's plans, Ford Motor Co. plans to install about 4 000 robots by 1990, less than GM but nevertheless an approximately tenfold increase of Ford's existing stock.

Spotwelding lines are presently the main work areas being robotised in the automobile industry. GM and most other producers are aiming at automating about 95-98 per cent of spotwelding operations. The spotwelding robots relieve human labour of a monotonous and arduous task, furthermore they are reliable and accurate providing consistent quality and higher productivity. The pay-back period for spotwelding robots is short – normally two to three years. Most automobile producers increased the utilisation of spotwelding robots significantly over the last few years and it is expected that by the mid-1980s most lines will be fully automated. Examples of company use of spotwelding robots include Toyota using about 400 robots with another 250 to replace existing welding facilities in 1982. By the end of 1982 most of the companies' spotwelding was expected to be automated and by 1983 an additional 200 spotwelding robots will complete the automation process. Nissan is presently using about 700 welding robots. As already noted, labour displacement by spotwelding robots is normally estimated at two welders replaced per shift so, for example, Chrysler replaced 200 welders over 2 shifts by 50 robots in one plant. At the same time, however, that plant's production rate increased from 50 cars an hour to 65. Fiat, which is increasing its use of robots by 30 per cent in order to increase the percentage of spotwelds carried out automatically to 98.5 per cent from 86 per cent has estimated that it will reduce direct labour time per body from 5 hours to 3.5 hours.

Robotised painting booths are another major area of application in automobile assembly. Besides eliminating labour from a health-hazardous area and increasing productivity, considerable savings are achieved in energy costs by eliminating the need for ventilation, and cost savings in paint are estimated at about 15 per cent. GM's painting booths are expected to use 8-10 robots each with an output of 60 cars per hour. Most automobile painting booths can handle several vehicle models and a range of colour changes.

Other examples of robot applications in the automobile industry include:

i) Fiat, which installed robots in 1978 in two automobile plants, boosted production by 15 per cent. The Renault plant at Douai uses 125 robots which are estimated as being 20 per cent more productive than manual labour. Output in the plant was expected to reach 80 cars per man by the end of 1982. Introduction of robots did not lead to labour lay-offs but the labour force is expected to decline over time through attrition.

ii) GM's new Lordstown plant which is presently producing 45-50 car bodies per hour is expected to attain a normal production rate of 75 car bodies per hour. The plant is extensively automated with welding and painting robots. In addition use is made of a robot-operated body inspection system to measure dimensions of J-car bodies in the assembly line. The system is also used to inspect stamped components and subassemblies.

iii) The Fiat-Comau Robogate system provides flexibility by allowing up to 4 different models to be manufactured in the same plant without interrupting the production process. This sytem reduces productions costs since no retooling or equipment modification is required and the cost of investment is spread over more models.

iv) Peugeot has automated its die-casting system for aluminium engine cyclinder blocks and steering column housings with the result that the production rate of engine blocks increased by 50 per cent and 35 per cent for steering gear housings. The automated systems include the use of a robot in the die-casting centre which led to labour saving of 3 workers per shift.

v) BL Cars use a robot for adhesive bonding of trunk lids, replacing 2 workers and increasing throughput by 100 per cent. Robots are also used to apply undersealing to car bodies and are used to test vehicles for watertightness.

vi) The use of flexible manufacturing techniques by Mitsubishi in Japan for the manufacture of its transmission units and engines reduced the required man-hours per unit from 8.8 hours to 2.3 hours and resulted in a 2.5 fold increase in monthly production without an increase in the labour force.

vii) G.M. (Chevrolet) will be bringing on stream in 1983 an automated engine assembly line which reduces labour requirements up to 50 per cent. The plant based on non-synchronous production methods uses robots and other flexible automation.

viii) The Chrysler Corporation is planning on modernising and automating its stamping plants. As part of this programme it is expected that by 1988 nearly 1 000 robots will be introduced, mainly in loading, unloading and transfer operations.

Outlook

The use of industrial robots, computer-aided manufacturing systems and other automated manufacturing equipment is expected to have a substantial impact on capital and labour productivity and on the cost structure of the automobile industry. In terms of labour:

i) there will clearly be a reduction of workposts. Renault have predicted that by 1990 12 per cent of assembly posts in automobile production will have been suppressed. For Volkswagen it has been estimated that 13 per cent of all workplaces can, from a technical point of view, be suppressed by robots. In the United States, experts have predicted that by 1990 nearly 50 per cent of final assembly for automobiles will be undertaken by programmable machinery. However, existing labour skills will be upgraded from unskilled to skilled labour;

ii) it could be argued that the increased utilisation of flexible automation might lead labour to moderate demands for increases in wages and in non-wage benefits. It is unlikely, however, that such concessions by labour in terms of wage increases would lead to a deferral of investment in flexbile automation given that pay back periods for flexible automation are already favourable, and that the expected trend is for declining machine costs.

iii) the flexibility offered by robots and CAM systems is often more important to producers than the labour savings since flexibility allows plants to produce profitably even at low levels of output.

In terms of capital:

i) the use of new automated production equipment is increasing equipment utilisation, production flexibility and easing maintenance of equipment, thus increasing capital productivity;

ii) the increased flexibility in addition to higher productivity of flexible automation will, over time, reduce investment requirements and facilitate product innovation.

iii) robots may not necessarily have higher productivity than specialised machinery, but their flexibility is important in situations where expected product variations are high and lot quantities variable.

While increased automation is viewed as important by producers, differences in degree in automation, by different producers or in different countries, is not generally cited as a prime reason for differences in productivity. Thus, for example, it has been estimated that the assembly time for a subcompact vehicle is 14 worker hours in Japan compared to 33 worker hours in the United States. This difference is not attributed to differences in degree of automation but rather to aspects such as efficient inventory control procedures in Japan (a process GM and Ford are examining closely), and better management-labour procedures. The increased adoption of flexible automation is being undertaken by the European, United States and Japanese producers so that it cannot be expected that automation per se will narrow international cost differentials.

The slowdown in demand growth for automobiles has increased the intensity of international competition and the drive by producers to maintain existing market shares. In turn this has led to significant attempts to improve productivity, improve vehicle performance and reliability and provide producers with the ability to rapidly modify design and components to reflect the latest technological advances. However, while significant employment repercussions in the industry can be expected, two considerations need to be taken into account. Firstly, in contrast to workposts already being robotised (welding, painting) which are health hazardous and monotonous, it can be expected that there will be greater union opposition to the introduction of robots in assembly posts. Secondly, extensive automation in automobile assembly requires a new generation of robots not yet commercially available.

Chapter IV

CONCLUSIONS

This report has briefly examined some long-term prospects for supply and demand in the automobile industry, an analysis that has highlighted the complexity of the factors influencing the industry's structure and development. The world automobile industry has entered a period marked by radical changes in terms of technology, production conditions and trade. This chapter aims to set out some of the main lines along which industrial strategies will probably develop and to indicate the role that international co-operation might play in helping to create a favourable environment for such changes.

The fundamental question at the OECD intergovernmental level is as follows: given the increasing and inevitable internationalisation of automobile production, how can governments facilitate positive adjustment in the automobile industry, while both paying due regard to the problems – particularly of a social nature – that may be posed by unduly abrupt adjustment, and avoiding distortions in international trade?

One principle must be set forth at the outset: neither the automobile industry nor governments themselves favour, or regard as an a priori necessity, intervention by the public authorities in the industry's problems, particularly where trading strategies are concerned. Governments' role should be as limited as possible, to ensure that the economic and international environment created makes it easier to resolve difficulties. It must also be recognised, however, that governments cannot dissociate themselves from an industry which is a major supplier of jobs, and is strategic, politically sensitive and a source of technological progress. It is therefore necessary to identify, at both national and international level, means of meeting these two requirements which may conflict in certain difficult periods.

Chapter II has shown that the world growth of demand for automobiles could well be around 2 per cent per annum for the whole period 1980-2000,. Growth will be lower in most industrialised countries where the saturation level is nearly reached and where replacement demand will be around 85 per cent of the total demand. It will be higher in industrialising and less developed countries. Chapter II and its methodological annex indicate clearly the inevitable uncertainties of such projections, which have to be regarded only as rather reasonable orders of magnitude. Some experts feel, however, that if very recent trends are taken into account, these estimates could prove optimistic.

Two main trends in future supply were discussed in Chapter III: these were the trends in technology and in adjustment strategies, including the choice of plant locations. The evolution in product technology probably will continue to be important but gradual; while that in process technology will be much more rapid. The progress made in the adaptation of products and manufacturing processes will, in the longer term, be a determining factor of competitiveness. It is in the interest of government to create general conditions favourable to this progress. They could accomplish this in many ways, in particular by facilitating co-operation between firms at national, regional and international levels, with a view to avoiding double work and waste in investment; by encouraging international basic research; and by helping to educate the labour force and the public about the technological progress needed.

Many governments have introduced some manner of regulations to deal with the problems arising from the use of automobiles (air pollution, noise, accidents, energy consumption, etc.). They should, however, be aware that these regulations place a heavy burden on industry, especially on the smaller producer of cars. This report has briefly drawn attention to the different problems that arise from the diverse regulations existing in many countries relating to the environment, safety, etc., and the long-term consequences, not only for trade, but also for the future structure of the industry. One element in increased international co-operation could be to seek greater harmonization to ensure that these regulations do not lead to major distortions in international trade.

The existing possibilities for increasing productivity in automobile plants by modernising manufacturing process, for instance by introducing robots, could throw some doubt on the longer term employment perspectives. However even if some automated production processes will be less labour-intensive than in the past, it is not the automatisation of production but rather the fall in demand and production which is mainly responsible for the present fall in employment in most producing countries. Robotisation is a means of reducing production costs in the automobile industry, but important cost reduction will also result from better management of stocks, and economies in materials, energy and cost of capital. Increasing utilisation of automated production processes will also have an impact on the qualifications needed by the labour force. With the revitalisation of economies, the revival of demand and the improvement of firms' competitiveness, the global employment prospects in the automobile and components industries of industrialised countries could, in the medium term at least, be stable and perhaps slightly favourable in some countries.

In the automobile industry, decisions regarding locations are based on a number of economic, industrial, commercial, social and policy factors. Two further factors seem to be essential in any location decision: the human factor, i.e. the type of possible industrial relations and their flexibility; and the policy factor, i.e. the possible intervention or interference of governments and the question of political stability. Generally, and in the longer term, the location trends in industry could move in two directions: on one hand the continuous process of modernisation (primarily on a scrap and build basis) in the main OECD industrialised countries, and on the other, the setting up of totally new capacities first in the newly industrialising countries and then in the developing countries. This is likely to lead to some degree of specialisation (based on the use of more sophisticated technologies) among manufacturers in the more industrialised countries and, at the same time, through a complex system of international industrial and trading links, to the development of several types of "world" or "regional" cars.

Chapter III also examined possible industrial adjustment strategies by analysing two extreme cases: the world car concept and the concept of technological specialisation. Clearly, the industrial reality is more complex, and most automobile producers will develop strategies for both increasing internationalisation and greater technological specialisation. Present economic difficulties and the protectionist trends in most producing countries do not facilitate implementation of the world car concept. Some form of internationalisation will however continue to increase, through technical, commercial and industrial co-operation.

If manufacturers wish to survive by deriving the maximum benefits from competition, they will have to move towards greater co-operation by developing the appropriate industrial, technical and trading relations. Such co-operation might develop at national, regional and world-wide levels and thus the occasional discussions about the number of firms which might survive would seem to be outmoded. Provided they continue to operate efficiently within the system of co-operation, most existing firms will probably continue to develop, perhaps not as independent individualised entities, but possibly in the context of very complex and highly decentralised groups. Technical and commercial co-operation agreements have already been seen to develop in recent years. This process can only become more marked over the next few years, whether within the context of the "world car(s)" or of some other technological development scenario.

In many cases, co-operation will have to go beyond the purely technical context. The establishment of joint enterprises offers evident advantages at both industrial and policy levels. At the industrial level, it facilitates transfers of technology, provides for more effective rationalisation of investment costs and possibly leads to better integration of marketing channels. At the policy level it can help prevent an increase in protectionist pressures. Long term, however, the local content of production probably will become a key issue in trade relations in the automobile industry, and there is some risk that more and more local content may be demanded. This would be detrimental to the future of the automobile industry as a whole. This is an area where the will, and the need, to engage in international discussion should make it possible to define common lines of approach.

The financial situation of many manufacturers deteriorated in 1981 and 1982. In the short term, the capability of firms to resist the crisis will depend both on the timing and strength of recovery, and on the producers' possibilities for lowering their manufacturing costs. The fundamental dilemma of producers is that investment should be launched immediately to maintain long-term competitiveness in products (in particular for fuel economies) and in manufacturing processes (in particular by increased automatisation), yet sales are falling and international competition is increasing. In 1981 and 1982, some companies announced investment reductions. If they are not counterbalanced by increased rationalisation in every area – structures, processes, etc., to ensure the adaptability and flexibility which would seem to be required in future years – and if a significant recovery does not appear – important problems could arise in the medium term for firms which have cash difficulties now.

An immediate consequence of the fall in automobile demand has been the emergence, in some countries, of excess capacity. This varies according to region: it is more substantial in the United States, where the increases in energy prices have led to structural change in demand, than in Europe; and it is practically non-existent in Japan. The problem of evaluating over-capacity in the automobile industry is extremely complex, and will become more so as the technological content of the product increases and the manufacturing process becomes more flexible. It is no longer possible to pose long-term analyses in terms of over-capacity, since the need for rapid adjustment to change has become a permanent factor in the world automobile situation. What seems to be over-capacity at a given time in a country may prove to be highly cyclical, transient and primarily related to factors such as the renewal of models or the deferred introduction of technical innovations.

Since manufacturers are steadily incorporating technological innovations into their products as soon as possible, and are endeavouring to keep abreast of trends in user demand, there is, and will continue to be, increasing uncertainty as to the proportional breakdown between cyclical and structural causes of over-capacity in the automobile sector. Furthermore, it is not at all clear that the problem of over-capacity in this industry is still presented in the same terms as in other more traditional industries. These reflections on the concept of capacity lead one naturally to think that the prime characteristic of the automobile industries in the future, and a condition for their survival, will be their ability to adapt to the changing demand and supply conditions. Increased flexibility will ease transitional periods but temporary excess capacity could still occur at specific locations. Governments should ensure, by multilateral appropriate information and discussion, that any emerging trade problems be solved without provoking protectionist chain reactions which would be harmful for all.

Automobile trade problems have not been dealt with directly in this report on long-term structural prospects of the industry. There is, evidently, a close link between trade and adjustment problems. The difficulties of 1980-81, for instance, resulted mainly from some delay in adjusting their production to the new more fuel efficient models sought by consumers, and from the time lag necessary to introduce new manufacturing processes to reduce production costs.

The issue of the appropriate structure of trade relations both in the short and medium term probably will be the main issue facing the automobile industry in the medium term as well as the short term. Having slid haphazardly into the present situation, where major trade flows are subject to restrictions, the danger is that this state of affairs will become permanent. This would be a significant blow to the international trading system built up since the war, and could exacerbate existing tensions in the industry and between countries. Moreover, the economic impact on the future structure of the industry would be profound, as adjustment to a changing international division of labour is frustrated.

In some rare cases, temporary trade measures may help a national car industry catch up on delays in technological investment. But temporary protection also isolates that nation's producers from international cost competition, and this is a long-term danger to the survival of that industry. Governments should thus evaluate the long-term impact of any temporary measures they feel they should implement. Multilateral exchange of information and discussion are among the means which could help in difficult periods to restore sound and balanced international competition.

Government and industry should reflect now on how to begin removing these restrictions as soon as a revival in the market facilitates appropriate industrial adjustment. This presupposes a political will to share the burden of adjustment to new world conditions. One possibility is simultaneous progressive lifting of restrictions in all markets. This cannot be done bilaterally; multilateral discussions are necessary.

It is important in this context that governments, in a spirit of international co-operation, follow closely and continuously the evolution of structural problems, so they may be solved before they become acute in trade terms. The criteria for positive adjustment agreed upon in the OECD suggest basic orientations for governments. In the case of automobiles, these criteria need to be discussed and confronted.

During this period of structural changes in the world automobile industry, it would seem essential to develop technical, industrial, inter-governmental structures for discussing possible future trends in the industry. It also seems necessary for governments to undertake exchanges of views so that, in a flexibile but continuing manner, they would be better able to assess emerging problems and solve them before they become acute.

* * *

To summarise the long-term prospects of the automobile industry in very few lines, it seems clear that, in a context of decreasing growth of world demand, producers will face rapid technological evolution in the product area and, more importantly, in the manufacturing process area. The quality and the speed of their responses will play a major role in determining their national and international competitivensss. To deal with these challenges, producers may adopt both a strategy of specialisation, mainly in the more technologically-advanced countries, and a strategy of internationalisation through technical, commercial and industrial agreements in the assembly and components fields to take advantage of any scale economy. Inevitable fluctuations in demand, whether of technological or economic origin, will cause temporary, and probably local or regional, excess capacity. Governments should ensure that the consequences of the imbalances are temporary and controlled so as not to hamper the rules of normal competition. Governments should also aim to restore normal competitive conditions in the automobile industry.

APPENDICES

Appendix A

STRUCTURAL CHANGES AND TECHNICAL INNOVATION
THE CASE OF ELECTRONICS

In the last few years, producers have increasingly used electronics and electronic components in cars as a result of the product innovations mentioned in Chapter II. The question arises as to whether automobile manufacturers should integrate "up-stream" and develop their own electronics manufacturing capacity or buy these components from outside suppliers.

A similar situation exists for the electronics suppliers who could move "down-stream" into auto-related activities; similarly, the existing suppliers of mechanical components can also integrate horizontally and expand their range of output to include electronic goods.

These decisions will affect the future development of the automobile industry, since greater product sophistication will probably result from the application of electronic components to cars. If design of these components is left to the electronics industry, then two results are implied. Firstly, the auto assemblers will lose some of their design capabilities to the electronics industry and may find themselves paying more for their electronic components than would be the case if they had been produced "in-house". Secondly, the strength of a country's electronics industry could play an important role in determining the survival of the country's auto industry.

Table 1. **Auto assemblers and electronic components (1981)**

Company	Engine control device	Electric control device	Safety systems	Passenger comfort	Driving aids
United States					
General Motors			Z X	Z X	Z X
AC Delco	Z	Z			
Ford					
EED	Z	Z		Z	Z
Chrysler	Z X	Z X	Z X		
Japan					
Toyota	Z	Z	Z	Z	Z
Nissan	Z				Z
Mitsubishi	Z X	Z X	Z X		
Europe					
Volkswagen	X				X
Renault	X	X	X	X	X
British Leyland		X	X	X	X
P.S.A.	X	X			X
Fiat	Z				

Type of electronic component : Z indicates actual production.
X indicates under development.
Note : For definition of categories used, see Chapter III.
Source : CREI, 1981.

If auto assemblers move upstream and establish their own electronics manufacturing capabilities, they can control design specifications and output levels; however such vertical integration requires investment, finance and new expertise.

In view of this analysis, upstream moves appear more likely by large "integrated" producers who can afford such investment. This might favour enterprises like General Motors, Ford, Volkswagen, Renault and Fiat as well as Nissan and Toyota. Such upstream integration can also represent greater diversification by auto assemblers. Auto firms could then enter the market for electronic components and automated manufacturing systems as sellers of advanced technology; Volkswagen and Fiat have already done so.

The third alternative is that existing components manufacturers extend into the production of electronic components, thereby maintaining their comparative advantage in component manufacture and preventing an encroachment by the electronics companies into their markets. Similarly, by obtaining an advantage in the production of electronic components, the components manufacturers may be able to improve their competitive position vis-à-vis the auto assemblers.

An idea of the extent to which the auto assemblers have moved upstream can be gained from Table 1. As of 1981, Japanese and American auto assemblers appear to have been the most committed to in-house production of electronic components. It is interesting to observe that only two companies, General Motors and Toyota, appear to have produced a complete range of electronic components in-house. Of these, only GM has developed its own design capability, Toyota relies on Japanese and American-licensed microprocessor technology.

Generally speaking, the European companies are still at the developing stage, and are concentrating less on engine regulatory devices than on electronic control and driving aid devices.

Table 2. **Auto components manufacturers and electronic components (1981)**

Company	Engine control device	Electric control device	Safety systems	Passenger comfort	Driving aids
United States					
Bendix	Z X				X
Eaton	Z			Z	Z
Europe					
Bosch	Z X	Z X	Z X		X
Ducellier		Z X			
SEV		Z			
Lucas	Z X	Z X	Z		
Smith					Z X
Veglia					Z X

Type of electronic component : Z indicates actual production.
X indicates under development.
Note : For definition of categories used, see Chapter III.
Source : CREI, 1981.

One reason for this might be that more of this work has been left to the traditional component suppliers like Bosch and Lucas; this trend can be seen in Table 2. This suggests that more upstream integration into electronic components production is taking place in Japan and the United States than in Europe. In the medium term, this might lead to a situation where technical change enhances the benefits of greater vertical integration in the United States and Japan, to the benefit of auto assemblers. In Europe, on the other hand, the components manufacturers look likely to extend their operations horizontally into the new area of electronics. This might result in a lower degree of vertical integration in the European industry than in the others.

Table 3 shows the links between the vehicle assemblers and their electronics suppliers and the components firms. The American electronics components firms appear to have the most diversified contacts with other companies. At the moment, it is difficult to predict whether the American companies will consolidate this advantage, or whether the European and Japanese companies will expand the number of their customers amongst the automobile assemblers.

Table 3. **Suppliers of electronics components technology in the automobile industry (1981)**

	United States							Japan	Europe			
	Intel	Texas Instruments	RCA	Motorola	Western Electric	Fairchild	Honeywell	Toshiba	Bosch	VDO	Renix	Thomson CSF
United States												
Ford[1]	×	×						×				
Chrysler[2]		×	×	×								
Japan												
Toyota[3]		×	×		×				×			
Nissan[4]						×	×		×			
Mitsubishi[5]				×								
Europe												
Volkswagen[6]						×			×	×		
Renault											×	
PSA[7]				×								×

1. Ford co-operates with Intel, Toshiba and Texas Instruments.
2. Chrysler buys components from these firms.
3. Toyota uses technology produced by these firms, handled by its Nippon Denso subsidiary.
4. Nissan has a joint venture with Bosch.
5. Second sourcing of components from Motorola.
6. Volkswagen co-operates with these firms.
7. Co-operation agreement.
Source : CREI.

108

WORLD CAR AND SPECIALISATION STRATEGIES: STATISTICAL ANALYSIS

Chapter III briefly outlined some possible "extreme" scenarios for industrial adjustment strategies, in particular the so-called "world car" strategy and the specialisation and/or technological divergence strategies. This appendix analyses two broad indicators of directions towards the world car concept or towards specialisation strategies to obtain an indication of present trends.

This report earlier concluded that if a "world" car concept is applied, the consequences might be that:

- model standardization would increase
- production would take place on a larger scale in more countries, including some outside of the traditional OECD producing areas
- trade in cars would be replaced by trade in components
- market shares of large "integrated" producers would expand at the expense of the specialist producers

The other main strategies described were those of technological divergence and specialisation. The consequences of these strategies might be that:

- model differentiation would increase
- production would continue to be concentrated in traditional manufacturing areas
- trade in cars would continue to be more important than trade in components
- the market shares of the smaller "specialist" producers could expand at the expense of the large "integrated" producers.

The following paragraphs attempt to assess recent trends and to indicate to what extent they correspond to the consequences outlined above.

In recent years, the number of countries with automobile manufacturing facilities has not increased greatly. The main non-OECD producers are Brazil, Mexico, Poland, Romania, the USSR, India and Argentina.

Table 1.   **Trends in assembly of cars in non-OECD countries**

'000 units in 1978

Countries experiencing an increase in assembly in the 1970s	Countries experiencing either no growth or reductions in assembly in the 1970s
Brazil (550)	
Columbia (32)	Argentina
Egypt (15)	India
Indonesia (30)	Algeria
Iran (123)	Angola
Ivory Coast	Burma
Mexico (250)	Chile
Malaysia	Israel
Nigeria (51)	Morocco
Peru (21)	Portugal
Philippines (35)	S. Africa
Thailand (17)	Tanzania
Trinidad (13)	Zambia
Venezuela (99)	

Source :   UN World Statistical Yearbook.

Leaving aside the centrally-planned economies, which have particular problems of their own, and noting that output in India and Argentina has stagnated, the only countries to have experienced recent and rapid growth are Brazil and Mexico. Of these two, only Brazil's production (around 550 000 cars) is above the minimum efficient size. Mexican production (around 250 000) is still on the low side.

This suggests that the recent shift of production away from the OECD countries has been smaller than is commonly supposed. Table 1 lists countries with increasing or decreasing/stagnant assembly volumes and shows that reductions in local assembly have taken place, and that average assembly volumes are low, and hence more expensive.

Another indicator of the growing internationalisation of automobile trade is the destination of exports from the OECD area. If decentralisation of production has in fact taken place, flows of components to non-OECD areas might have increased. Similarly, if incomes in non-OECD areas rose, this might lead to an increase in the proportion of OECD passenger vehicle exports to non-OECD areas.

As Table 2 shows, there was relatively little change in the overall pattern of OECD trade between 1970 and 1980. The only noticeable difference was in components trade, where a higher proportion of OECD exports was delivered to non-OECD areas in 1980 than in 1970. Bearing in mind the results shown in Tables 1 and 2, it can be concluded that the shift in components trade towards the non-OECD countries is largely a result of tariff and non-tariff barriers to trade in finished cars. The flow of components to non-OECD areas is used mainly to service local markets, and not re-exported.

Table 2. **Destination of exports**

OECD as a whole

Total transportation equipment 78	1970	1975	1975
Total to OECD	77.3	72.1	75.2
OECD to non-OECD	22.7	27.9	24.8
Passenger Vehicles SITC 781			
To OECD	86.3	87.3	86.5
To non-OECD	13.7	12.7	13.5
Commercial Vehicles SITC 782			
To OECD	56.4	41.7	56.3
To non-OECD	43.6	58.3	43.7
Components SITC 784			
To OECD	76.2	75.5	71.3
To non-OECD	23.8	24.5	28.7

While increases in production have occurred in some non-OECD countries, the scale clearly is still below the considered minimum efficient size. The only "new" countries to have emerged with significant levels of domestic production are Brazil and Mexico, and there is much to suggest that they are special cases rather than the leaders of a trend that will be followed by others. Automobile production is still overwhelmingly concentrated in the traditional OECD producing areas: the United States, Canada, France, Germany, Japan, Italy, Sweden and the United Kingdom.

This indicates that although there has been some shift in production away from the traditional OECD areas, the shift has not been fully consistent with a successful and widespread application of the "world car" concept.

The Composition of Automotive Trade

Another conclusion reached in assessing adjustment strategies was that, subject to some qualifications, there would be either:

a) a considerable increase in the components trade; or
b) no relative increase in the components trade, depending on the extent of the application of the world car concept.

Post-war changes in of the composition of international trade in the road vehicle industry demonstrate quite clearly that there are marked differences in the structure of trade between different countries. The differences in the structure of the trade flows within the OECD are sufficiently great to suggest that simple global generalisations should be sought only with great caution. In the following section these differences are examined in more detail[1].

There have been remarkably few changes in the aggregate proportion of exports accounted for by passenger cars and components in automotive trade within the OECD. Approximately half the value of exports has been accounted for by passenger vehicles, and about 30 per cent by components. There does not appear to have been either short- or long-run shifts in these proportions. However, these overall figures mask some considerable changes in the position of individual countries, which will be examined below.

It is useful to distinguish among three groups of countries: first, those with above-average representation of passenger vehicles which persisted between 1961 and 1980. This group consists of Japan and F.R. Germany. The second group includes countries with a falling representation in automobile exports and rising share of components exports. France and Italy are in this category. Finally, the third group, namely the United Kingdom and the United States, has an above-average representation of components in automotive exports.

Japan and F.R. Germany

As Tables 3 and 4 show, car exports are "over-represented" in Japanese automotive exports. This trend changed substantially between 1962 and 1970, when Japan's earlier, below-average, share of automobile exports changed so that car exports formed a very large share of total Japanese automotive exports. This above-average share of cars in exports became more marked in the decade 1970-1980.

By contrast, there has been a noticeable "under-representation" of components in the automotive exports of Japan. In the decade 1970-1980 there may have been a slight tendency for this lower-than-average share to increase slightly.

These figures indicate the relatively great extent of the dependence of Japanese exports on finished cars. In contrast to other countries, there is no sign that this trend is being reduced. The low proportion of components exports in automotive trade suggests that the Japnese component industry is not yet internationally established, and serves the domestic market to a much greater extent than that of other countries. The small share of components exports may be attributable to the flow of spare parts necessary for service and repair purposes. If the concentration in the Japanese components industry increases this pattern may change.

The Federal Republic of Germany also has a higher-than- average share of passenger cars in its automotive exports. There is some indication that this share declined between the 1960s and 1970s, but then remained relatively constant between 1975 and 1980. A similar development has occurred in components exports. In the 1960s these were "under represented". In the 1970s, the share in Germany converged with the OECD average, but in 1980 it was still less than for the OECD as a whole.

Japan and F.R. Germany are the only two countries to share the characteristics of a relative "over representation" in passenger cars, and an "under-representation" in components. According to the assumptions listed above, these industries deviate substantially from a "world car"-type pattern.

France and Italy

These two countries share a number of features. Their above-average performances in car exports has fallen rapidly since the 1960s, and much more rapidly than that of F.R. Germany. France's share of car exports is still greater than the OECD average, but in Italy car exports now form a below average share of automotive exports. Their situation in components is also similar: from having a below average share, they now both have an above average share. The rate of increase has been quite striking for Italy.

In these countries, two trends can be observed. First, their respective shares of cars in automotive exports tend now to be much closer to the OECD average. Second, the international orientation of trade in components has become much clearer in both countries.

The increasing share of components in French and Italian exports superficially appears to support the "world car" hypothesis. More detailed analysis suggests that there are several reasons for this development,

1. The main analysis is given in Tables 3 and 4, and a few words of explanation are necessary to explain the method used. The average proportion of trade in road vehicle exports for the OECD as a whole was calculated by summing the total of passenger vehicles (SITC 781), commercial vehicles (SITC 782) and components exports (SITC 784), and calculating what the individual proportions of each element were, based on this sum. The total arrived at differs from SITC 78 road vehicles, since it excludes motorcycles and special purpose vehicles (and vehicles not elsewhere specified).

From this it was possible to establish average OECD structure of automotive trade. The deviation of country (i)'s share of a particular component from the OECD average for year "t" was then worked out and expressed as a percentage of the OECD average. Thus, a figure like − 50 (row 2, column 1 of Table 3) shows that the share of exports of 781 in country (i)'s automotive trade was 51 per cent less than the OECD average. The figures shown in Tables 3 and 4 therefore give an idea of the extent to which a country is either relatively over- or under-represented in its export trade in a given category of goods. The figures in row 1 are for convenience only; they give the average share of passenger vehicles (Table 3) and components (Table 4) exports in automotive exports for the OECD as a whole. The figures in rows 2 to 7 do not refer to either growth rates or absolute values but to the deviations from the OECD average. Some general remarks will be made about trends in the OECD as a whole, before proceeding with more detailed country analyses.

Table 3.   Changes in composition of exports of cars (SITC 781) compared to OECD average

OECD average[1] SITC 781	1961	1965	1970	1972	1973	1974	1975	1976	1977	1978	1979	1980
	54	54	55	58	57	53	50	53	54	53	53	52
Japan[2,3]	−50	+ 3.7	+18.1	+22.4	+21.0	+18.9	+24.0	+22.6	+22.2	+18.9	+22.6	+25.0
F.R. Germany	+25.9	+31.4	+16.36	+15.5	+14.0	+15.1	+10.0	+ 9.4	+16.7	+17.0	+13.2	+11.5
France	+31.4	+31.4	+27.2	+24.1	+24.6	+20.8	+22.0	+18.9	+13.0	+13.2	+17.0	+ 7.7
Italy	+37.0	+25.9	+20.0	+17.2	+14.0	+13.2	+14.0	+11.3	+ 5.6	+ 1.9	0	− 9.6
United Kingdom	− 5.1	− 9.2	−20	−31.0	−35.1	−34.0	−38	−39.6	−42.6	−37.7	−45.3	−46.2
United States	−59	−51	−52	−50.0	−43.9	−39.6	−38	−39.6	−38.9	−45.3	−37.7	−44.2

1.   Figures in row 1 show the proportion of passenger car vehicle exports as a % of a total consisting of SITC 781 + 782 + 784.
2.   Figures in rows 2 to 7 show the difference between country i's average and the OECD average for passenger cars or components, i.e.

$$\frac{x - x_i}{x} \times 100 = Z$$

Where $Z > 0$, then that country's share is greater than the OECD average (shown in row 1).
Where $Z < 0$, then the country's average is less than that of the OECD. The averages refer to the shares in automotive trade and not to absolute amounts. The figures, therefore, do not add up to 100.

112

Table 4. Changes in composition of exports components SITC 784

	1961	1965	1970	1972	1973	1974	1975	1976	1977	1978	1979	1980
OECD average[1] SITC 784	29	32	30	29	30	31	29	29	28	29	29	28
Japan	− 5.1	−62.5	−70	−72.4	−70.4	−64	−65.5	−72.4	−67.8	−62.1	−65.5	−67.9
F.R. Germany	−41	−40	−20.0	−20.7	−16.7	−16.1	−13.8	−13.8	−14.2	−13.8	−10.3	− 7.1
France	−44	−40	−26	−24.1	−26.7	−19.4	−13.8	10.3	0	0	− 3.4	+10.7
Italy	+41.3	−40	−16.7	−24.1	−20	−16.1	− 6.9	− 3.4	+10.7	+ 6.9	+10.3	+32.1
United Kingdom	+27	0	+50	+55.2	+56.7	+58.1	+65.5	+62.1	+71.4	+48	+79.3	+89.3
United States	+75.8	+90.6	+96	+96.6	+80.0	+67.7	+62.1	+72.4	+82.1	+54	+75.9	+96.4

1. Figures in row 1 show the proportion of passenger car vehicle exports as a % of a total consisting of SITC 781 + 782 + 784.
2. Figures in rows 2 to 7 show the difference between country i's average and the OECD average for passenger cars or components, i.e.

$$\frac{x - x_i}{x} \times 100 = Z$$

Where $Z > 0$, then that country's share is greater than the OECD average (shown in row 1).
Where $Z < 0$, then the country's average is less than that of the OECD. The averages refer to the shares in automotive trade and not to absolute amounts. The figures, therefore, do not add up to 100.
Note : Detailed analysis of exports under SITC 784 shows that it consists largely of the mechanical and structural components necessary for car production. It also includes the exports of engines and chassis. However, it excludes the export of internal combustion engines alone as well as much electrical equipment and peripheral equipment such as carburettors and electric generators. Tyres are also excluded.

113

and that not all of them are consistent with the development of "world car" production. Indeed, some of these trends are also consistent with the market specialisation strategy mentioned above.

It is useful to distinguish between three variations of growth in the share of components in automotive exports. The first of these is the French variant, wherein component transfers are largely intra-company and, to that extent, support the world-car hypothesis. The bulk of this trade takes place between France and Spain and, it could be argued, is a direct result of previous foreign direct investment. The pattern follows that pioneered by Ford.

The second is the German variant where the flows of components induced by foreign investment have not been so large. This suggests that the foreign subsidaries are more independent of the domestic German market: they receive fewer components from Germany and export fewer to it. There appears to be a much higher interdependence between the Spanish and EEC markets than between the Latin American producers and the EEC. There is some evidence that Latin American exports and imports of components are primarily confined to the American continent and take place between North and South America. The German variant suggests that German foreign investments are less integrated into a "world-car" concept than is the case for the French producers.

The third variant is that of the Italian industry, which shares a number of features with both the American and British industries. In Italy, there has been a rapid growth in the share of components in automotive trade, without a corresponding increase in foreign investment. This indicates that components are not being sold to subsidiaries of Italian companies, nor are old assembler-component supplier relations simply being extended to other markets. It appears that Italian components are being sold on world markets as low cost components to other independent companies.

United States and United Kingdom

In contrast to the other countries considered, the most striking feature about the pattern of US and British trade is the great over-representation of components and under-representation of passenger vehicles. This pattern has remained reasonably constant for the US industry, while there have been more significant changes in the British industry.

The above-average share of components in US automotive trade is largely caused by the extensive components trade with Canada. Components are sent to Canada for assembly into cars, some of which are then exported to the United States. This great regional concentration in the trade pattern once more emphasises that great caution is needed when interpreting international trade data. The present structure of US components trade is probably less the result of the production of any "world car" and more the result of trading agreements between the United States and Canada.

The "under representation" of US passenger vehicle exports draws attention to the regional specialisation of US automobile production. The product differences between American and non-American cars limited the extent of foreign demand for US exports.

The British pattern of development is not quite the same as United States'. During the 1960s, the "under representation" of car exports was less pronounced than in 1980. The figures in Table 3 show a relative decline in UK passenger car exports, so that the next deviation (downwards) from the OECD average doubled between 1970 and 1980. This trend is largely the result of the difficulties – including product design, low investment, difficulty in meeting delivery dates and industrial relations – that beset the industry at that time. There is also some evidence that important changes in export-sourcing policy by the US companies operating in the United Kingdom contributed to the low average share of passenger vehicles in automotive exports[2].

Table 4 shows a steady rise in the share of components in British automotive trade to levels which occcasionally exceeded those of the United States. Special factors have accounted for this development; and those associated with US development, namely regional specialisation, are not relevant. The high share of components in British automotive exports did not stem from British automobile industry investment abroad, which would have induced flows of British components; there was, in fact, no direct auto investment abroad in that period. The specialisation in components may be due to the slow growth, or fall in the size of the British market, and in particular to the lower performance of the domestic vehicle assemblers. This has created excess capacity in the components industry, which has thus turned to exporting.

This suggests that both the British and, to a lesser extent, the Italian industries have been drawn into a components specialisation strategy by the weakness of components demand from domestic producers. These components are then sold competitively to other assemblers in foreign markets.

There are basically two ways of viewing the strong component specialisation of the British, US and Italian automotive industries. The difference between them lies in the presence or absence of extensive foreign investment in other countries.

According to the world car concept, increases in components trade should largely take the form of intra-company transfers between the parent company and its subsidiaries as well as between subsidiaries. This

2. Black, 1981.

is partly true for the US but one should not forget the regional specialisation of the North American car market. However, the flow of components between the United States and other areas is indicative of some world car-type production.

The British and Italian concentration on trade in components grew in the absence of foreign investment by their domestic industries in foreign markets[3]. The trade in components has, therefore, largely taken the form of inter-company transfers. This type of trade is more similar to a specialisation of those countries' automotive sectors in components production, and is more supportive of a market specialisation strategy than of world car production.

The persistence of this trend does suggest that market specialisation in components is a viable strategy in the medium term. Even though the transfers are probably more of an inter- than of an intra-firm nature, they may be indicative of a vertical "disintegration" of production. This means that, for cost reasons, vehicle assemblers may be more willing to buy out a higher proportion of components than was previously the case.

There are, however, a number of factors which might adversely affect this trend toward market specialisation in components. Domestic demand levels could recover, absorbing spare capacity in the components industry and reducing exports. Competitive pressures could favour component producers located closer to the vehicle assembler. This would follow the pattern of the Japanese industry. If this is the case, the specialist component producers in distant locations would probably have to invest abroad in new facilities closer to the assembler. This would lead to a substitution of foreign production for components exports from the United Kingdom and Italy. Finally, trade restrictions could make international components specialisation unfeasible by limiting specialist components suppliers to their domestic markets.

Market Shares of the "Specialist" Producers (i.e. producers active in some sectors of the market)

Apart from these trends in the composition of automotive trade another indicator of the type of adjustment strategy being pursued is the competitive situation of different companies on the world market. At the beginning of this section it was argued that a marked increase in the market shares of "integrated"[4] producers would suggest a shift in production towards the manufacturers of "world" cars. "Integrated" producer includes companies like General Motors, Ford, Volkswagen, Renault, Peugeot, Fiat, Toyota and Nissan. Greater market shares of these companies could be attributed to a variety of factors, but one of them would be their ability to offer well-designed cars at economical prices. Their superior price competitiveness would be one indication of the success of their cost-reducing world car strategy.

Table 5.   « Specialist »[1] producers - production

	1969	1970	1971	1972	1978	1979	1980
Alfa Romeo	104 305	107 989	123 309	140 595	219 499	207 514	219 571
Lancia	31 556	44 542	52 789	41 778	52 462	60 459	110 756
Volvo/Daf	60 732	67 262	78 087	87 396	64 881	90 204	80 779
Rolls Royce	n.a.	n.a.	n.a.	n.a.	3 348	3 343	3 108
Jaguar/Rover/Triumph	197 121	200 771	220 863	218 557	187 010	148 519	80 601
Honda	232 704	276 884	215 256	235 248	652 920	706 375	845 514
Mitsubishi	127 812	246 422	260 981	222 890	628 886	528 555	659 622
Saab	61 219	73 980	72 960	83 997	72 516	83 758	65 754
Volvo	181 668	205 991	214 438	233 965	181 740	212 782	169 566
American Motors	242 898	276 127	235 669	279 132	164 352	184 636	164 725
BMW	136 491	158 618	163 832	181 964	311 793	337 981	341 031
Daimler Benz	256 713	280 419	284 230	323 878	403 707	435 711	445 495
Porsche	15 292	16 757	10 905	14 503	36 879	36 011	28 622

1. See note to paragraph 37.
   The list of companies here represents the main « specialist » producers. The main criterion for inclusion was that the company concerned concentrated on supplying some part of the market only. The list understates the amount of « specialist » production since many smaller companies, mostly with production of less then 5 000 per annum, have been omitted.
   Source :   VDA Tatsachen und Zahlen. Various editions.

3.   This refers to foreign investments in other OECD countries, or in Brazil and Mexico. There has been some investment by the Italian industry, but not on a sufficiently large scale for it to compare with developments of the French and German industries, let alone the scale of foreign operations supported by the American firms.
4.   An integrated producer refers to a vehicle assembler producing a range of vehicles, such that it is represented in all major market segments. This would mean that the company sells in the segments under 1 000 cc., 1 000-1 300 cc. 1 300-1 700 cc., 1 700-2 500 cc and above 2 500 cc. A "specialist" producer sells only in some of the segments; one should not be surprised, given the above definition, to find, within the "specialist" category, some companies with a relatively large output.

An alternative scenario is that the "specialist" rather than the "integrated" producers managed to increase their market shares. This would indicate their ability to offer a wide range of product characteristics for a given price in a given market segment, as compared to the standardisation offered by "integrated" producers. It would also indicate that product differentiation was more successful than product standardization.

Output figures for a number of specialist producers are presented in Table 5. They show production by company for selected years from 1969 to 1980. Comparing the 1969 to 1980 production, it can be seen that output of the Italian, German and Japanese "specialists" has increased considerably. Production levels of US and British "specialists", have declined, while output levels among the Scandinavian specialists have remained stable. Total output of this group of companies has risen steadily so that it exceeded 3 million units in 1979, and continued to increase in 1980 despite an overall decline in world automobile output that year.

Table 6 shows the share of the specialists' output in world, and major OECD country production[5]. There has been a steady rise in the specialist share of world production from just over 7 per cent in 1969 to nearly 11 per cent in 1980. The rise has been more pronounced when compared to output within the major OECD countries. Here, the share increased from nearly 8 per cent in 1969 to 13 ½ per cent in 1980. These figures indicate that there has been no tendency for the integrated producers to reduce the specialists' market share. On the contrary, the specialists have managed to consolidate and expand their market positions during this time, particularly in the major OECD countries. This is of particular interest, since it suggests a growing appreciation of product differentiation by consumers in the high income OECD markets and indicates that product differentiation and market specialisation has been a successful adjustment strategy in the last few years.

There are some additional reasons for thinking that this trend may continue in the future. Technical developments, particularly in product innovation, have led to a more intensive use of capital equipment. Robotics and other forms of automation permit greater production flexibility for the same amount of fixed capital. This allows shorter production runs without incurring the previously high additional cost penalties. In its turn, this implies that the advantages of large-scale economies may be declining, thus improving the competitiveness of the smaller "specialist" producer. These companies frequently have been more willing to engage rapidly in product innovation, since this has formed part of their product differentiation strategy.

Table 6 also shows that 85 to 90 per cent of the automobiles produced in the OECD are manufactured by the larger "integrated" companies. The rate of change of market shares is not rapid enough to suggest that these larger companies are not going to play a major role in the future. Nevertheless, the inroads made by the specialists into the "integrated" companies' market shares may be less quantitatively and more qualitatively significant, since they could disproportionately affect the integrated producers' profitability. The specialists may be concentrating their attention on the most profitable market segments to the detriment of the longer-run expansion plans of the integrated producers.

Table 6.   « Specialist » producers' share of market

	1969	1970	1971	1972	1978	1979	1980
World production	22.74	22.57	26.15	27.52	31.68	31.49	29.21
Major OECD[1]	20.89	20.33	23.55	24.47	26.39	25.92	23.63
Specialist Production[2]	1.65	1.95	1.93	2.06	2.99	3.03	3.21
Specialist Share - World	7.26	8.64	7.38	7.49	9.44	9.62	10.99
Specialist Share - OECD	7.9	9.59	8.20	8.42	11.33	11.69	13.58

1. OECD consisting of EEC, Japan, United States, Canada and Sweden.
2. « Specialist » production (see Table 5).

5.   Major OECD countries consist of Canada, the EEC, Japan, Sweden and the United States.

BRIEF BIBLIOGRAPHY

W.J. Abernathy, *The Productivity Dilemma: Roadblock to Innovation in the Automobile Industry*, Johns Hopkins University Press, 1978.

W.J. Abernathy, K.B. Clark and A.M. Kantrow, "The New Industrial Competition", *Harvard Business Review*, September-October 1981.

W.J. Abernathy, J. Dopico, B.H. Klein and J.M. Utterback, A Dynamic Approach to the Problems of the Automobile Industry, paper presented to the First International Policy Forum on the Future of the Automobile, Pennsylvania, USA, 1981.

M.L. Anderson, Structural Changes in the World Auto Companies: the Emerging Japanese Role, Society of Automotive Engines, 1982.

M.L. Anderson, *Strategic Organisation of the Japanese Automotive Groups*, M.L. Anderson, Cambridge, Mass. 1981.

M.L. Anderson, Retrenchment and Reconstruction in the US Auto Industry: Labour, Management and International Implications, paper presented to the *Second International Policy Forum on the Future of the Automobile*, Hakone, Japan, 1982.

M.L. Anderson, Financial Restructuring of the World Auto Industry, paper presented to the *Second International Policy Forum on the Future of the Automobile*, Hakone, Japan, 1982.

W. Bernhardt (1980): Alternative Kraftshoffe und Energien, Methanol und Athenol, Auto 88, VW, AG.

A.P. Black (1981): Long Run Theories of Economic Growth and Development with Reference to the American and British Automobile Industries, Unpublished Ph.D. thesis. University of London.

K.B. Clark, Competition, Technical Diversity and Radical Innovation in the US Auto Industry, Harvard Business School Working Paper HBS 82025, 1982.

R.B. Cohen, International Market Positions, International Investment Strategies and Domestic Reorganisation Plans of US Automakers, paper presented to the *Second International Policy Forum on the Future of the Automobile*, Hakone, Japan, 1982.

Daimler-Benz (1979): Energieeinsparung. Gewichtsreduzierung am Automobile. Krafthand 52.

EEC, *The European Automobile Industry:* Commission Statement, Brussels, 1981.

R.H. Hayes and W.J. Abernathy, "Managing our Way to Industrial Decline", *Harvard Business Review*, July-August 1980.

G. Heyl (1980): Kunstoffmotor aus den USA in Motorrad 22.

Ch. Hildenbrandt (1980): Raum- und Gewichtsoptimierung im Automobilbau; Aufbau, Auto 88, VW AG.

D.T. Jones, *Maturity and Crisis in the European Car Industry: Structural Change and Public Policy*, Sussex European Paper No. 8, Sussex European Research Centre, Brighton, 1981.

D.T. Jones, Technology and Competitiveness in the Automobile Industry, paper presented to the *Second International Policy Forum on the Future of the Automobile*, Hakone, Japan, 1982.

D.T. Jones, (1982, b) *Adjustment strategies and policy issues in the Automobile industry*, SPRU, Brighton.

B.H. Klein, Dynamic Economics, Harvard University Press, 1977.

D. Kleinstuber (1979): Energieeinsparung durch optimale Fahrzeuggestaltung, Umshau 79. 8 edition.

Abdelaziz Mahjoub, (1981): Energiesparmassnahmen im Strassenverkehr, Unpublished Diplom arbeit. Institut für Fahrzeugtechnik. Technical University of Berlin.

L. de Mautort and Associates, Differences in Production Costs in Seven Great Automobile Manufacturing Countries, CEPII working paper, Paris.

OECD, *Car Ownerhsip and Use*, 1981.

OECD, *Main Economic Indicators. Historical Statistics* – 1960-1979, Paris.

US Department of Transportation, *US Automobile Industry 1980,* Washington, 1981.

R. Wilkens (1980): Gewichtseinsparung durch thermoplastische Chemiewerkstoffe im Kraftfahrzeuge; ATZ 82, 3.

J.P. Womak and D.T. Jones, The Competitive Significance of Government Technology Policy in the Auto Sector, paper presented at the *Second International Policy Forum on the Future of the Automobile,* Hakone, Japan, 1982.

ARGUS, Annual Statistics

Various companies' annual reports.

OECD SALES AGENTS
DÉPOSITAIRES DES PUBLICATIONS DE L'OCDE

ARGENTINA – ARGENTINE
Carlos Hirsch S.R.L., Florida 165, 4° Piso (Galería Guemes)
1333 BUENOS AIRES, Tel. 33.1787.2391 y 30.7122

AUSTRALIA – AUSTRALIE
Australia and New Zealand Book Company Pty, Ltd.,
10 Aquatic Drive, Frenchs Forest, N.S.W. 2086
P.O. Box 459, BROOKVALE, N.S.W. 2100

AUSTRIA – AUTRICHE
OECD Publications and Information Center
4 Simrockstrasse 5300 BONN. Tel. (0228) 21.60.45
Local Agent/Agent local :
Gerold and Co., Graben 31, WIEN 1. Tel. 52.22.35

BELGIUM – BELGIQUE
Jean De Lannoy, Service Publications OCDE
avenue du Roi 202, B-1060 BRUXELLES. Tel. 02/538.51.69

BRAZIL – BRÉSIL
Mestre Jou S.A., Rua Guaipa 518,
Caixa Postal 24090, 05089 SAO PAULO 10. Tel. 261.1920
Rua Senador Dantas 19 s/205-6, RIO DE JANEIRO GB.
Tel. 232.07.32

CANADA
Renouf Publishing Company Limited,
2182 ouest, rue Ste-Catherine,
MONTRÉAL, Qué. H3H 1M7. Tel. (514)937.3519
OTTAWA, Ont. K1P 5A6, 61 Sparks Street

DENMARK – DANEMARK
Munksgaard Export and Subscription Service
35, Nørre Søgade
DK 1370 KØBENHAVN K. Tel. +45.1.12.85.70

FINLAND – FINLANDE
Akateeminen Kirjakauppa
Keskuskatu 1, 00100 HELSINKI 10. Tel. 65.11.22

FRANCE
Bureau des Publications de l'OCDE,
2 rue André-Pascal, 75775 PARIS CEDEX 16. Tel. (1) 524.81.67
Principal correspondant :
13602 AIX-EN-PROVENCE : Librairie de l'Université.
Tel. 26.18.08

GERMANY – ALLEMAGNE
OECD Publications and Information Center
4 Simrockstrasse 5300 BONN Tel. (0228) 21.60.45

GREECE – GRÈCE
Librairie Kauffmann, 28 rue du Stade,
ATHÈNES 132. Tel. 322.21.60

HONG-KONG
Government Information Services,
Publications/Sales Section, Baskerville House,
2/F., 22 Ice House Street

ICELAND – ISLANDE
Snaebjörn Jónsson and Co., h.f.,
Hafnarstraeti 4 and 9, P.O.B. 1131, REYKJAVIK.
Tel. 13133/14281/11936

INDIA – INDE
Oxford Book and Stationery Co. :
NEW DELHI-1, Scindia House. Tel. 45896
CALCUTTA 700016, 17 Park Street. Tel. 240832

INDONESIA – INDONÉSIE
PDIN-LIPI, P.O. Box 3065/JKT., JAKARTA, Tel. 583467

IRELAND – IRLANDE
TDC Publishers – Library Suppliers
12 North Frederick Street, DUBLIN 1 Tel. 744835-749677

ITALY – ITALIE
Libreria Commissionaria Sansoni :
Via Lamarmora 45, 50121 FIRENZE. Tel. 579751/584468
Via Bartolini 29, 20155 MILANO. Tel. 365083
Sub-depositari :
Ugo Tassi
Via A. Farnese 28, 00192 ROMA. Tel. 310590
Editrice e Libreria Herder,
Piazza Montecitorio 120, 00186 ROMA. Tel. 6794628
Costantino Ercolano, Via Generale Orsini 46, 80132 NAPOLI. Tel. 405210
Libreria Hoepli, Via Hoepli 5, 20121 MILANO. Tel. 865446
Libreria Scientifica, Dott. Lucio de Biasio "Aeiou"
Via Meravigli 16, 20123 MILANO Tel. 807679
Libreria Zanichelli
Piazza Galvani 1/A, 40124 Bologna Tel. 237389
Libreria Lattes, Via Garibaldi 3, 10122 TORINO. Tel. 519274
La diffusione delle edizioni OCSE è inoltre assicurata dalle migliori librerie nelle
città più importanti.

JAPAN – JAPON
OECD Publications and Information Center,
Landic Akasaka Bldg., 2-3-4 Akasaka,
Minato-ku. TOKYO 107 Tel. 586.2016

KOREA – CORÉE
Pan Korea Book Corporation,
P.O. Box n° 101 Kwangwhamun, SÉOUL. Tel. 72.7369

LEBANON – LIBAN
Documenta Scientifica/Redico,
Edison Building, Bliss Street, P.O. Box 5641, BEIRUT.
Tel. 354429 – 344425

MALAYSIA – MALAISIE
University of Malaya Co-operative Bookshop Ltd.
P.O. Box 1127, Jalan Pantai Baru
KUALA LUMPUR. Tel. 51425, 54058, 54361

THE NETHERLANDS – PAYS-BAS
Staatsuitgeverij, Verzendboekhandel,
Chr. Plantijnstraat 1 Postbus 20014
2500 EA S-GRAVENHAGE. Tel. nr. 070.789911
Voor bestellingen: Tel. 070.789208

NEW ZEALAND – NOUVELLE-ZÉLANDE
Publications Section,
Government Printing Office Bookshops:
AUCKLAND: Retail Bookshop: 25 Rutland Street,
Mail Orders: 85 Beach Road, Private Bag C.P.O.
HAMILTON: Retail Ward Street,
Mail Orders, P.O. Box 857
WELLINGTON: Retail: Mulgrave Street (Head Office),
Cubacade World Trade Centre
Mail Orders: Private Bag
CHRISTCHURCH: Retail: 159 Hereford Street,
Mail Orders: Private Bag
DUNEDIN: Retail: Princes Street
Mail Order: P.O. Box 1104

NORWAY – NORVÈGE
J.G. TANUM A/S Karl Johansgate 43
P.O. Box 1177 Sentrum OSLO 1. Tel. (02) 80.12.60

PAKISTAN
Mirza Book Agency, 65 Shahrah Quaid-E-Azam, LAHORE 3.
Tel. 66839

PHILIPPINES
National Book Store, Inc.
Library Services Division, P.O. Box 1934, MANILA.
Tel. Nos. 49.43.06 to 09, 40.53.45, 49.45.12

PORTUGAL
Livraria Portugal, Rua do Carmo 70-74,
1117 LISBOA CODEX. Tel. 360582/3

SINGAPORE – SINGAPOUR
Information Publications Pte Ltd,
Pei-Fu Industrial Building,
24 New Industrial Road N° 02-06
SINGAPORE 1953, Tel. 2831786, 2831798

SPAIN – ESPAGNE
Mundi-Prensa Libros, S.A.
Castelló 37, Apartado 1223, MADRID-1. Tel. 275.46.55
Libreria Bosch, Ronda Universidad 11, BARCELONA 7.
Tel. 317.53.08. 317.53.58

SWEDEN – SUÈDE
AB CE Fritzes Kungl Hovbokhandel,
Box 16 356, S 103 27 STH. Regeringsgatan 12,
DS STOCKHOLM. Tel. 08/23.89.00
Subscription Agency/Abonnements:
Wennergren-Williams AB,
Box 13004, S104 25 STOCKHOLM.
Tel. 08/54.12.00

SWITZERLAND – SUISSE
OECD Publications and Information Center
4 Simrockstrasse 5300 BONN. Tel. (0228) 21.60.45
Local Agents/Agents locaux
Librairie Payot, 6 rue Grenus, 1211 GENÈVE 11. Tel. 022.31.89.50

TAIWAN – FORMOSE
Good Faith Worldwide Int'l Co., Ltd.
9th floor, No. 118, Sec. 2,
Chung Hsiao E. Road
TAIPEI. Tel. 391.7396/391.7397

THAILAND – THAILANDE
Suksit Siam Co., Ltd., 1715 Rama IV Rd,
Samyan, BANGKOK 5. Tel. 2511630

TURKEY – TURQUIE
Kültur Yayinlari Is-Turk Ltd. Sti.
Atatürk Bulvari No : 77/B
KIZILAY/ANKARA. Tel. 17 02 66
Dolmabahce Cad. No : 29
BESIKTAS/ISTANBUL. Tel. 60 71 88

UNITED KINGDOM – ROYAUME-UNI
H.M. Stationery Office,
P.O.B. 276, LONDON SW8 5DT.
(postal orders only)
Telephone orders: (01) 622.3316, or
49 High Holborn, LONDON WC1V 6 HB (personal callers)
Branches at: EDINBURGH, BIRMINGHAM, BRISTOL,
MANCHESTER, BELFAST.

UNITED STATES OF AMERICA – ÉTATS-UNIS
OECD Publications and Information Center, Suite 1207,
1750 Pennsylvania Ave., N.W. WASHINGTON, D.C.20006 – 4582
Tel. (202) 724.1857

VENEZUELA
Libreria del Este, Avda. F. Miranda 52, Edificio Galipan,
CARACAS 106. Tel. 32.23.01/33.26.04/31.58.38

YUGOSLAVIA – YOUGOSLAVIE
Jugoslovenska Knjiga, Knez Mihajlova 2, P.O.B. 36, BEOGRAD.
Tel. 621.992

Les commandes provenant de pays où l'OCDE n'a pas encore désigné de dépositaire peuvent être adressées à :
OCDE, Bureau des Publications, 2, rue André-Pascal, 75775 PARIS CEDEX 16.

Orders and inquiries from countries where sales agents have not yet been appointed may be sent to:
OECD, Publications Office, 2, rue André-Pascal, 75775 PARIS CEDEX 16.

67306-01-1984

OECD PUBLICATIONS, 2, rue André-Pascal, 75775 PARIS CEDEX 16 - No. 42723 1983
PRINTED IN FRANCE
(70 83 04 1) ISBN 92-64-12523-X